Receive His Love

Song of Songs
for Personal Reflection and Group Conversation

Aletha Hinthorn

cometothefire.org

Receive His Love
Copyright © 2012 Come to the Fire Publishing
Published by Come to the Fire Publishing
PO Box 480052
Kansas City, MO 64148
cometothefire.org
Library of Congress Cataloging in Publication Data:
ISBN 978-0-9838316-6-2
Printed in the United States of America

Library of Congress Cataloging in Publication Data:
ISBN 978-0-9838316-4-8
Printed in the United States of America

"I belong to my lover, and his desire is for me"
(Song of Songs 7:10).

Table of Contents

Introduction 7

Yearning for Love 11

The Loving Eyes of Jesus 17

Discovering the Beauty of Jesus 25

A Banner of Love 32

The Lover's Invitation 37

The Consequences of Little Foxes 44

The Celebration 51

What Jesus Admires 55

Jesus Finds No Flaw 61

Our Turning Point 68

The Cost to Follow Jesus 73

The Beauty of Jesus 83

Jesus Delights in His Garden..93

Compelled by Love...100

Lovingly Abandoned to Jesus..108

Poured Out Love...114

The Seal of Love..124

Appendix A: Voices from the Past...132

Appendix B: Scriptures for Worship.......................................135

Appendix C: Names and Descriptions of God................139

Appendix D: Women Role Models.....................................142

Introduction

If you know Christ, but desire deeper intimacy with Him, this book is for you. No book of the Bible better describes our journey to intimacy with Christ than Song of Songs. It tells the story of a maiden who had a sincere desire to be closer to her Lover. At first she focuses on her own enjoyment of Him and what He can do for her. By the end of the Book, she understands how delightful she is to Him, and her one desire is to please Him.

You may be surprised to learn, as I was, that in the last 3000 years, this book has received more attention than any other book of the Bible. Aqiba, a first-century rabbi, stated, "The whole world is not worth the day on which the Song of Songs was given to Israel, for all the Scriptures are holy, but the Song of Songs is the Holy of Holies."

Throughout the centuries, Song of Songs has been one of the most loved books of the Bible. During the dark days before the Protestant Reformation when John Huss led his small bands of persecuted Christians, this book was frequently read, quoted, and memorized. It comforted them greatly.

Then after the Reformation, in the time of bitter persecution when the Presbyterian Church was birthed, Song of Songs again became one of the most often quoted books. It sustained the spirits of persecuted men and women throughout Europe.

Spurgeon said, "Let me prefer this book above all others for fellowship and communion." When Charles Finney entered into a deep love relationship with Christ, he said, "The language of the Song of Solomon was as natural to me as my breath."

For centuries both Jewish people and Christians have considered this book to be a song about our relationship with God. Amazingly, God looks upon His relationship with us in nuptial terms. Song of Songs has also been recognized as speaking of romance between husband and wife. This is an acceptable interpretation, but that relationship is a shadow of the reality. Since it's beyond us to know the depths of God's love but not beyond us to grasp marital love, God describes His love by comparing it to marriage. As Ephesians 5 tells us, the relationship of husband and wife is to reflect that of Christ and His bride.

Seventeenth century Puritan Thomas Watson said, "There is a closer union in this holy marriage than there can be in any other. In other marriages, two make one flesh, but Christ and the believer make one spirit: 'But he who is joined to the Lord is one spirit with Him'" (I Corinthians 6:17).

"This spiritual union brings in more astonishing delights and ravishments than any other marriage relationship is capable of. The joy that flows from the mystic union is unspeakable and full of glory (I Peter 1:8)." (See Appendix A to read what others have said about our nuptial relationship with God.)

Song of Songs is Christ's ecstatic description of His passion for you and me. It is a love document to help us grasp the truth that He is passionate about us and we bring Him great joy.

Isaac Watts wrote, "Our marriage union with husband or wife cannot be more clear, more sure, more matter of fact, than our oneness with Christ and our enjoyment of that oneness. Joy! Joy! Joy! He whom we love is ours!"

This book is properly understood as we learn to decipher its symbolic language. Jesus often used symbolic language when speaking of Himself. For instance, when He said in John 10, "I am the door," we understand that we enter eternal life through trusting in Him. And when He says in Revelation 3 that He stands at the door and knocks, He is again using "door" as a symbol.

So in trying to understand the imagery, rather than merely using our creative imaginations to interpret the symbols, we look to the Bible and ask what other places these words and concepts are used. Usually the Bible defines and interprets itself. For instance, God used the word "neck" repeatedly when He spoke of Israel as being a rebellious "stiff-necked" people. It means they set their will against God. Proverbs 3:3 tells us to never let love and faithfulness leave us but to bind them around our neck. From these and other Scriptures, the neck seems to have something to do with the will.

I'm grateful to other authors who have written on Song of Songs. Mike Bickle has compiled an excellent set of teaching notes that are available on the Internet. Other authors I have gleaned from include Dennis Kinlaw, Hudson Taylor, Watchman Nee, Richard Wurmbrand, Esher Shoshannah, Jessie Penn-Lewis, and numerous commentaries.

I've used The New International Version unless otherwise indicated. As stated in a footnote of that version, "In some instances the divisions and their captions are debatable." At times, I have interpreted it differently as have many commentaries.

Frequently the psalmist inserted the word "Selah," a word that means "suspension (of music)" or "pause, think on this." In this book, most of the verses conclude with a "Selah" followed with a comment to encourage you to pause and reflect on what God is saying to you.

When the maiden reached spiritual maturity, she exclaimed with joyful confidence, "I belong to my lover, and his desire is for me" (7:10). May her words become our happy song.

Yearning for Love

The maiden longs for Jesus' kisses—evidences of His affections—so she can delight in His love. She knows, though, that unless He draws her, she will lack the desire necessary to seek Him with all her heart.

1:1 The song of songs, which is Solomon's (NKJV).

Solomon wrote 1005 Songs (1 Kings 4:32), but the Holy Spirit inspired him to name this book using the ultimate superlative—the Song of Songs. The book preceding the Song of Songs is Ecclesiastes in which Solomon described every possible thing that could give purpose to life. His conclusion? Life apart from God has no meaning. He used the word "meaningless" 28 times in Ecclesiastes to describe the fulfillment of enjoying everything "under the sun."

Then in this Song, Solomon introduces us to the maiden who discovers a Bridegroom who loves her unconditionally. His loving heart satisfies her completely. She discovers the purpose for which she was created—to joyfully and wholeheartedly abandon herself to Him and receive His love in return. Discovering Jesus' love for her ignites her love for Him and becomes the passion that drives her life.

Beloved

1:2 Let him kiss me with the kisses of his mouth—for your love is more delightful than wine.
The first thing the maiden says is, "Let him kiss me with the kisses of his mouth." She yearns for more intimate communion with her Lord and expresses her desire by asking for kisses of His mouth. This verse gives the foundation for all that occurs in this book.

From the beginning, the rabbis associated Deuteronomy 8:3 with this passage: "Man does not live on bread alone but on every word that comes from the mouth of the LORD." For 3000 years, the rabbis would speak of the kisses of God's mouth like this: "The kisses of the Torah are what we long for."

Origen, an early Church Father, said that when the Jewish Church prayed, "Let him kiss me with the kisses of his mouth" they were expressing a longing for a closer revelation. It was as though they were asking, "How long shall He send me kisses by Moses and the prophets? I desire the touch of His own lips"—a longing expressed in Hosea 2:16: "When that day comes," says the LORD, "you will call me 'my husband' instead of 'my master'" (NLT).

Our journey to true intimacy with God will begin as the maiden's did. We, too, will desire Him; we will hunger for His Word to become sweet to us. Jesus is always attracted by those who long to know Him better; He is not waiting for us to be perfect.

Jesus is the living Word. In fact, Revelation 19:13 declares, "The name by which he is called is The Word of God" (ESV). Much of our Bible study can be compared to receiving kisses from the prophets. We glean insights from Bible study teachers, books, and ministers, but we could cry with the maiden, "Let Him kiss me!"

When a fresh insight comes directly to us from Jesus, the Living Word, it is like a kiss on our spirits. It gives us life! "They are not just idle words for you—they are your life" (Deuteronomy 32:47). Our spiritual lives thrive by feeding on that which comes from the mouth of God. (Deuteronomy 8:3; Matthew 4:4)

We do not speak of kissing the lips of Jesus—that would be sacrilegious. But there is a mystical meaning, and when we begin to grasp it, we will be enthralled with the beauty of receiving His affection through the Word. We may be in the midst of a crisis or have a special need and He gives us a promise from His Word and it is as satisfying as a kiss on the lips. His divine kiss, His Word spoken into our spirits, is the communication of His love and favor.

She begins with the words "Let him." It is important to invite Him. Ask God's Spirit to fall on you with a fresh passion to hear Jesus speak to you through Scripture. True intimacy with God begins when His Word becomes precious to us.

Wine represented the best pleasure the world could offer to bring happiness. Whatever the world declares makes you glad, Jesus' love for you is incredibly sweeter and His Word infinitely more to be desired.

If you want to draw nearer to Jesus, ask Him to increase your desire to spend time with His Word. When you act on any small desire you have, He will reward you by giving you the best gift—more desire.

Selah: Has God ever given you a kiss—a verse from Scripture that was just what you needed that day?

yes!

Describe what you think it means to receive a kiss from Jesus when you read His Word. *He sees me & meets my deepest need & I am truly satisfied & at peace.*

When you read the Bible, begin as this maiden did and ask for a kiss from His Word. Jesus loves to hear us use His Word in prayer and praying Scripture often draws us near Him. See Appendix B.

1:3 Pleasing is the fragrance of your perfumes; your name is like perfume poured out. No wonder the maidens love you!

She asked to be spiritually kissed and immediately was blessed with a revelation concerning Jesus' name. Thinking on His Name is as refreshing as opening a bottle of the finest perfume. We do not see or take hold of a fragrance, but it makes an impact on us.

His Name speaks of His works, character, kindness, power, and wisdom. I was praying about a concern and realized I had no clue how God could answer my prayer. Then I remembered that one of His Names is El-Roi: the strong One who sees. My El-Roi sees the circumstance better than I do. He sees ways to answer that I could not fathom. He sees the best time to answer. Thinking on His Name El-Roi was like a sweet fragrance to my spirit enabling me to leave my care with Him.

The maiden has noticed others' affection for Him and now she understands how right they are to adore Him. Perhaps seeing others' love for Him is what gave her a longing to enter into that same enjoyment.

Selah: His name is above all names. His name <u>heals</u> (Acts 3:6), <u>saves</u> (Matthew 1:21; John 1:12), <u>delivers</u> (Acts 16:18), <u>leads</u> (Psalm 31:3), <u>protects</u> (Psalm 124:8), <u>forgives</u> (Psalm 79:9). Pray using names of God from Isaiah 9:6. Consider what Philippians 2:9-10 means.

For to us a child is born, to us a son is given, & the government will be on His shoulders. And He will be called Wonderful Counselor, Mighty God, Everlasting Father, Prince of Peace. Of the increase of His government & peace there will be no end. Isaiah 9-6,7

1:4 Draw me after you; let us run. The king has brought me into his chambers (ESV).

She's eager to be alone with her Lover, yet she's dependent upon His calling her. She longs for communion with Him, but she realizes that coming into intimacy with Him begins when the Spirit places the desire in her heart, so she prays, "Draw me after you."

How dependent we are on Him to draw us to Himself! His drawing power becomes our pursuing power. If He does not draw, we have no desire to pursue. "No one can come to me unless the Father who sent me draws him" (John 6:44).

[margin handwriting: Ask to discuss in class. Pursue further. Draw & pursue]

What a perfect prayer for us to pray when we long for a closer relationship with the Lord or even when we awaken in the mornings and find little desire to read the Word or pray. We plead, "Jesus, draw me to Yourself."

Selah: Jesus longs for intimacy with you, but He waits for your invitation. Why do you think we can not come near Him unless He draws us? *Because we are still self-reliant instead of God-reliant*

Ask Him to draw you and to put a deep desire to be near Him in your heart. What might be evidences He is answering? *My increasing desire to spend more & more time w/ Him in prayer, bible study & nature*

Friends

We rejoice and delight in you; we will praise your love more than wine.

The Friends are believers who have yet to be gripped with holy passion for Jesus. They are sincere and true believers but less mature in their love. They love the Giver for His gifts. When we become eager for a closer walk with Jesus, those less spiritually mature notice. They, too, begin to change. These friends began to echo her thoughts.

The one thing that will draw immature believers into pursuit of Jesus is seeing our hearts abandoned to Him. As we long to know Him better, others are stirred to a new level of devotion.

Selah: Do you know someone who is totally in love with Jesus? How has their love of Jesus influenced your pursuit of Jesus? ① Beth Koch - Pilates Instructor ② influenced me to be more outspoken in my love for Jesus to those I come in contact with, whether it Beloved be friends, family, acquaintances or strangers.

How right they are to adore you!

She says this to Christ. She is enthralled with His presence and declares it is right for all the world to adore Him.

The Loving Eyes of Jesus

The Spirit now deals deeply with the maiden because she sincerely asked Him to draw her to Himself. When she came close to the King, she suddenly acknowledged:

1:5 Dark am I, yet lovely, O daughters of Jerusalem, Dark like the tents of Kedar, Like the tent curtains of Solomon.

When God exposes us, we are growing in our journey. The closer we get to Jesus, the more clearly we see ourselves as He sees us. Things we once overlooked, we now see with new eyes in His presence.

The maiden admits she is "dark" even though she is "lovely." Others saw her as lovely as the tent curtains of Solomon, but there were things hidden within her that were not right. She had a revelation of her unsubmitted soul. Her mind, intellect, emotions, and will had not all been brought under the control of the Spirit.

"Woe to me!" Isaiah cried when He was in God's presence. "I am ruined! For I am a man of unclean lips" (Isaiah 6:5). Many desire their selfish nature to be dealt with in secret and are not willing to be as honest before others as they are before God. It appears, though, she was not trying to hide what He was revealing to her. <u>Freedom comes when our pride is broken and we humbly confess what the Spirit reveals.</u>

After Jesus revealed Betty's self-centeredness, she admitted, "I fought off a desire to turn away from these painful revelations about myself...Seeing my self-righteousness and pride made me want to hide my head in shame. I felt awed by the exposure of my selfish, arrogant nature. When the tears of repentance came, there were comfort and reassurance in His manner." After His Presence left, "Everything was unchanged outside of myself. Inside I was different."

Selah: Intimacy with Jesus is conditional. Pray the psalmist's prayer in Psalm 139:23-24 and ask the Holy Spirit to show you if there is anything "offensive" in your life. Wait before Him. What does He say?

1:6 Do not stare at me because I am dark, because I am darkened by the sun. My mother's sons were angry with me and made me take care of the vineyards; my own vineyard I have neglected.

For the maiden, being "darkened by the sun" refers to those things she did apart from God's direction. The phrase "under the sun" means "apart from God" and emphasizes that life without God has no meaning. "When I surveyed all that my hands had done and what I had toiled to achieve, everything was meaningless, a chasing after the wind; nothing was gained under the sun" (Ecclesiastes 2:11).

Search me, o God, + Know my heart; test me + Know my anxious thoughts. See if there is any offensive way in me, + lead me in the way everlasting Psalm 139:23-24

18

Instead of seeking His pleasure, she had been driven by others' expectations. Perhaps her mother's sons (her Christian brothers) took full advantage of her fervency and zeal and overworked her.

In her desire to please them, she became sidetracked and allowed her own vineyard (the garden of her heart) to suffer. Still, she realized she could not blame others that she had grown cold. Cultivating her own vineyard was her daily responsibility. Now her desire to be looked up to or honored has fled. She is weary of merely doing what others expect instead of passionately pursuing Jesus.

We can easily be distracted from our devotion to Jesus while working in the church. Like Martha, others may expect us to help with dinner—or whatever their project is —and misunderstand us when we don't sense God asking us to join their efforts. When asked to volunteer, we may feel obligated to do anything and everything.

The enemy loves to get us so busy in legitimate projects that we find no time for intimate fellowship with the Bridegroom of our heart. After a while, we grow tired and wonder what happened to the joy we experienced earlier.

The fruit we bear while not abiding in Christ will be fruit of the flesh and not of the Spirit. We may find we are working for Him but without Him.

Selah: Do you participate in activities because of others' expectations rather than out of love for Jesus?
Not any more, praise be to God!

Which of your priorities take time away from your pursuit of Jesus? none now, by God's grace & my daily examination, confession of sin & Surrending of my will for His will.

How will you reorder your priorities to cultivate your own vineyard? Continue to resist the temptation of man's approval over God's approval 19 in my life.

1:7 Tell me, you whom I love, where you graze your flock and where you rest your sheep at midday. Why should I be like a veiled woman beside the flocks of your friends?

The maiden recognizes that she wants to be a lover of Jesus, not just a worker for Him.

Regardless of the cost, she must live "unveiled"—without hiding anything from Him. Only then would He be free to bring her into the intimacy she desires. She wants nothing between them.

Now that she has begun longing for Him, she is aware that she needs rest. Before coming to Him, she overlooked this need and kept busy. She focused on the flocks and not on the Shepherd. Their needs caused her to overlook her own needs.

Jesus knows we need rest. When the crowds were coming and going around His disciples, He said to them, "Come with me by yourselves to a quiet place and get some rest" (Mark 6:31). Jesus still invites us to come with Him to a quiet place. Before deciding for ourselves how to find rest, we must go to Him first. We often think of doing whatever is easy—flip on the TV, check the news on the Internet, see what our Facebook friends are doing. Even if the activity in itself is not sinful, our greatest need may not be met.

Women had just walked out of my house after a draining Women Alive planning session and soon more women would be coming for a Bible study. I was weary and about to sit down with a cup of coffee when the thought came, *Why not just kneel down in the presence of the Lord?* As I knelt there, Scripture flowed into my mind that totally refreshed me.

The maiden's question expressed her desire for Jesus. "Where do You feed Your flock?" Is it in Your house? Then I will go. Is it in private prayer? Then I will pray. Is it in Your Word? Then I will read it diligently. Tell me where

You feed Your flock, <u>for wherever You are is where I will</u>
<u>lie down as your sheep.</u>

    Selah: When you need rest for your soul, where do you
turn? Do you sometimes feel your need for Him but not
know what to do?

— Nature + rest

    What helps to bring you to a place where You sense
you are near Him? Consider Psalm 100:4.

*Enter His gates w/ Thanksgiving & His courts
with praise; give thanks to Him & praise His Name.*

Lover

**1:8 If you do not know, most beautiful of women, follow the
tracks of the sheep and graze your young goats by the tents of
the shepherds.**

    Jesus quickly responds with loving admiration when
we look honestly at ourselves. He calls her the "most
beautiful of women" despite her describing herself as
unlovely. Instead of rebuking her for being too busy and
too distracted, He admires her. The more we are willing to
admit the darkness He shows us in ourselves, the more
beautiful we are to Him.

    He directs her to follow the footsteps of <u>those truly</u>
<u>surrendered leaders who consistently have the fruit of the</u>
<u>Spirit in their daily walk.</u> Fellowship with them and follow
their footsteps. While serving with others who are tending
His flock, she will find Him. <u>She is to limit her</u>
<u>responsibilities to what God gives her.</u>

    Selah: Jesus asks you to follow truly surrendered
believers. What qualities will they exhibit?

*Vulnerability, availability, humility, peace,
simpleness & NO arrogance!*

1:9 I liken you, my darling, to a mare harnessed to one of the chariots of Pharaoh.

His words surprise her. Although He knows she has neglected Him, He does not rebuke her as many would. He delights in her seeking heart and makes no mention of her being too busy for Him or too distracted.

In ancient poetry the horse was used as an emblem of beauty and inner strength. A mare harnessed to one of Pharaoh's chariots must be totally obedient. Its only role would be to carry the King wherever he wanted to go.

He says, "You have no idea how beautiful you are to me, my darling." His terms of endearment give her confidence He delights in her. He is infinitely kind to those who fail. "The Lord is full of tenderness and mercy" (James 5:11).

Horses were used in Solomon's day for battle. "The LORD Almighty will care for his flock...and make them like a proud horse in battle" (Zechariah 10:3). Because of her passionate desire to draw near Him, He envisioned her as having great strength ready to do amazing things.

That is the way He sees each of us when we begin to draw near Him. He knows that He will use us to carry burdens for others and do exploits for Him. He is excited about our prospects.

Gideon saw Himself as totally unqualified to lead the Israelites in battle. "My clan is the weakest in Manasseh, and I am the least in my family" (Judges 6:15).

But the angel of the LORD announced, "The LORD is with you, mighty warrior."

Someone may say, "But I've been a prostitute and have HIV." He says, "I see you as my redeemed child who has a heart of compassion for people infected with HIV."

Another may say, "But I've failed to bring my children up to fear You." He says, "I see you as an effective intercessor whose prayers will accomplish My purposes in their lives."

You may say, "But I've tried and failed to be faithful in prayer and Bible reading." He says, "I see you as one who has discovered the joy of coming to Me daily."

He calls her darling, or my love. There may be someone reading this thinking "Surely He does not call me His darling, His beloved. I should not even have been born." If so, God has a special word for you. After David committed adultery with Bathsheba and she became pregnant, he had her husband Uriah murdered to cover his sin. He married Bathsheba and they had a son—a son who would not have been born if his father had not committed adultery and murder. They named him Solomon which meant peace. Perhaps David thought that now he could have peace because God had given him this son despite his sin.

But even more remarkable is the special name God gave baby Solomon. God "sent word through Nathan the prophet that they should name him Jedidiah (which means 'beloved of the LORD')" (2 Samuel 12:25). He is the only one with that name in the Bible. It's as though God wanted to send a special message to any one who may feel that they should not have been conceived. God says, "You are my Jedidiah; you are my delight; I love you."

Selah: Write what comes to mind when you ask Jesus to show you how He sees you.

1:10 Your cheeks are beautiful with earrings, your neck with strings of jewels.

1:11 We will make you earrings of gold, studded with silver.

Eastern women wore a cord at the forehead with strings of precious stones hanging down over the cheeks. He promised the maiden, "Your cheeks are beautiful with what you have provided, but I can make you even more beautiful!"

He likes the personality He gave each of us, but no matter how naturally kind and gracious we are, when our kindness is Spirit-filled, it is as different as Divinely-made gold earrings studded with silver are to those we fashion ourselves. He is eager to "beautify the humble with salvation" (Psalm 149:4 NKJV).

He will make your best efforts to be kind, loving, joyful, patient, and good even more beautiful with graces He will supply.

Selah: Can you think of a time God helped you be kind or patient when those would not have been your natural responses? Was there a Scripture (a kiss from His Word) that helped you?

All the time, esp. in workplace. My natural inclination to injustice is prideful. It is only w/ great effort on my part to surrender my flesh to allow the H.S. to flow through me. A dying to myself allows the H.S. to flow freely

Discovering the Beauty of Jesus

The maiden freely and boldly spoke to Jesus of her love as an example for us. Hymn-writer Isaac Watts desired that people would frequently "express the fervor of devout love to our Savior, in the style of the Song of Solomon."

Beloved

1:12 While the king was at his table, my perfume spread its fragrance.

Her presence was a perfume to Him. The Hebrew for "perfume" is spikenard, which was an expensive fragrance made from a plant being crushed and is the emblem of humility.

When Jesus was at His table, Mary of Bethany "came with an alabaster jar of very expensive perfume made of pure nard. She broke the jar and poured the perfume on His head. Some of those present were saying indignantly to one another, 'Why this waste of perfume? It could have been sold for more than a year's wages and the money given to the poor.' And they rebuked her harshly" (Mark 14:3-5).

Her expensive perfume "wasted" on Jesus expressed her love that was willing to sacrifice all. It was exceedingly precious to Jesus. "Leave her alone," said Jesus. "Why are you bothering her? She has done a beautiful thing to me." He promised that the memory of her humble expression of love to Him would never be forgotten. Her poured out love accomplished more than she knew.

♡ He has not changed. He treasures our poured-out love. We can express our love to Him in hundreds of ways throughout the day. When we say about our daily activities, "I am doing my best for You, Jesus," or "This is for You, Jesus," we're offering Him a precious fragrance.

We have an open invitation to God's table. "Here I am! I stand at the door and knock. If anyone hears my voice and opens the door, I will come in and eat with him, and he with me" (Revelation 3:20). Learn to enjoy His fellowship.

Selah: Begin to practice the presence of God, and give Jesus the joy of the fragrance of your perfume. Often couples in love sit quietly savoring the enjoyment of each other's presence. Love Him by taking time to silently think about Him.

Reflect on these words: "I will love You, O LORD, my strength" (Psalm 18:1).

1:13 My lover is like a sachet of myrrh lying between my breasts. NLT

Hebrew women often wore little bags or bottles of myrrh, a sweet smelling fragrance, suspended from their necks and hanging down under their dress. It continually gave a delightful aroma. But the fragrance of myrrh was significant. Myrrh has a sweet smell but a bitter taste. It signifies suffering and speaks of Jesus' death on the cross. It was an expensive perfume used by the wealthy as a burial spice. Psalm 45:8 tells us that Jesus' robes were fragrant with myrrh.

The maiden embraces Him to her heart as she meditates on the cross and begins to understand the price He paid to draw her to Himself. She never wants to forget the cost of the fragrance. It is so delightful to dare to think of this One who suffered so much to be her Lover.

Selah: What comes to your mind when you think about the price Jesus paid for you? Thank Him for the love that caused Him to die so He can enjoy your fellowship.

Grievous gratitude. I grieve at what I cost Him. I am grateful that He loved me that much as to give His life for me.

1:14 My lover is to me a cluster of henna blossoms from the vineyards of En Gedi.

Henna comes from a Hebrew word that means atonement. Jewish teachers in ancient times believed the phrase "a cluster of henna blossoms" referred to the Messiah. They translated it "a man who atones for all." Henna was both beautiful and fragrant. The fragrance of Christ's atonement for all our sins is indeed a sweet fragrance.

How wonderful that we have One who "understands our weaknesses, for he faced all of the same testings we do, yet he did not sin" (Hebrews 4:15 NLT). He is still carrying our sorrows. "It was our weaknesses he carried; it was our sorrows that weighed him down. And we thought his troubles were a punishment from God, a punishment for his own sins! But he was pierced for our rebellion, crushed for our sins. He was beaten so we could be whole. He was whipped so we could be healed." (Isaiah 53:4-5 NLT).

After someone said something to me that left me feeling rejected, Jesus spoke to my spirit, "Let me carry your burden. Let that fall on me. I am your burden-bearer." After that thought went through my mind, I noticed I no longer felt the rejection. This Scripture came to me: "The insults of those who insult you have fallen on me" (Romans 15:3).

He shed His blood to deliver us from all that saddens our lives. He replaces anger with peace, unforgiveness with love, sadness with joy, worry with confident expectation. He provides healing for the wounded and counsel for the confused. _suffering_ _atonement_

The rich fragrances of myrrh and henna express the sweet presence of Christ that is now possible for us to enjoy. "Christ in you, the hope of glory" (Colossians 1:27) translates into "Christ in you, the joyful and confident expectation of a most glorious life."

Selah: Is there anything you need to release to Jesus? Ask Him to take your hurts and pains and replace them with His love, joy, peace. Repeatedly remind yourself, "The insults of those who insult you have fallen on me" (Romans 15:3).

Do you recall a time when He has replaced your sorrow with His peace?

Lover

1:15 How beautiful you are, my darling! Oh, how beautiful! Your eyes are doves.

She has just expressed how precious He is to her, and He is so elated with her that He repeats, "How beautiful you are, my darling! O how beautiful!" We have little idea of how precious our loving words are to Jesus. He rejoices over all of us who take time to tell Him how very much He means to us. "As a bridegroom rejoices over his bride, so will your God rejoice over you" (Isaiah 62:5).

Doves' eyes are mentioned six times in the Song. He is describing a quality that Jesus intensely wants to cultivate in her. A dove's eyes have no peripheral vision. So when it fixes its gaze upon its mate, it is not distracted by any activities around it. It is often referred to as being a "love bird." Also, a dove has only one mate in its life, so to have doves' eyes is to be loyal.

Our having "dove's eyes" indicates that we possess a spiritual awareness and can be easily led by Him, for we are close enough to see which way His eye is looking. In her daily life with a myriad of decisions, she would look into His eyes. The more she did so, the more she understood His desires and knew what to do.

Selah: "But my eyes are fixed on you, O Sovereign LORD" (Psalm 141:8). What do you think it means to have your eyes fixed on Jesus in your daily life?

A life surrendered

1:16 How handsome you are, my lover! Oh, how charming! And our bed is verdant.

1:17 The beams of our house are cedars; our rafters are firs.

He praises her beauty, but in her eyes it is He who is beautiful. The more she sees of Jesus' beauty, the more she adores Him. She is seeing Him as her charming lover and rejoicing in the thought of spending her life in fellowship with Him.

Her place of rest with Him is completely satisfying! Verdant means green, fresh, and lush. She rests in His presence enjoying His love. There is no better resting place than Christ. "He makes me lie down in green pastures" (Psalm 23:2).

They continually speak of their love and joy in each other modeling the kind of sharing Jesus wants to have with us.

In these early stages of growing in intimacy with her Lover, she focuses on what He is to her, not what she is to Him. This is appropriate for now, but her focus will change. She will become aware of His rights to enjoy her and that she exists for Him alone. She will see herself as the one He desires.

Selah: Notice that she is listening to Him. After the kiss of His words to her, she seems to have reached a new level of spiritual maturity. Why is listening to what Jesus says in the Word the secret to our spiritual growth?

It is living bread for
Spiritual nourishment & growth

Beloved

2:1 I am a rose of Sharon, a lily of the valleys.

The rose of Sharon and the lily of the valleys are very common flowers. She says she is a common, ordinary flower, one of thousands. She wonders why He would see beauty in her. Why is He singling her out? "I am just one of so many, Lord. What do you see in me?" She thinks humbly of herself and uses an unassuming expression.

We, too, can think that such a love relationship with Jesus may be only for those more special than we, but we are each equally precious in His sight.

Selah: Jesus had good words to say about the lowly lily. "See how the lilies of the field grow. They do not labor or spin. Yet I tell you that not even Solomon in all his splendor was dressed like one of these" (Matthew 6:28-29). Read Matthew 6:25-34. What words would you use to describe the care Jesus offers?

indescribable
extravagant
thirst quenching

30

2:2 Like a lily among thorns is my darling among the maidens.

He takes her comparison of herself and gives it a remarkable turn. He declares that others do not compare with her. Because she has sought to come closer to Him, He receives her as though she is the most special one in the world.

He is saying to her (and to us): "I see the hunger of your heart. I am moved by your request when you first prayed, 'Draw me.' You were expressing a longing for something more than your present experience, and it turned My heart and desire toward you."

He wants us to know that He views us as beautiful when we are desiring more of Him even though we may feel undeserving. He would rather we trust in His love than doubt His mercy.

Selah: How do you respond to this truth: "Your desires to draw near Jesus are His most precious possessions"?

w/ Relief + awe.

A Banner of Love

Jesus wants us to enjoy the "kiss" of daily communion with Him. We are changed, just as she was, as we experience the wonder of His love.

Beloved

2:3 Like the finest apple tree in the orchard is my lover among other young men. I sit in his delightful shade and taste his delicious fruit. NLT

The apple tree is thought to refer to what was formerly called "Persian apple"—a fruit that was very fragrant and bore fruit in all seasons. She compares Him to a beautiful tree that allows her the pleasure of sitting close to Him and enjoying His refreshing presence at any time.

Jesus was her protective shade. "The LORD is your shade at your right hand" (Psalm 121:5). She found Him to be her shadow from the heat and refuge from the storm.

32

Sitting implies she was resting quietly meditating upon Him and feeding upon His Word. Spending her time in this way was her delight.

Selah: She obviously spent time just enjoying His presence. How important do you think it is to do that? What helps you focus on delighting in Him?

1. Very important, crucial to deepening our relationship
2. Being quiet in nature, reading scripture, praying, listening

Consider recording your insights, memorizing, meditating. (See *How to Read the Bible so It Changes Your Life* for suggestions.)

2:4 He has taken me to the banquet hall, and his banner over me is love.

Young's literal interpretation is, "He hath brought me in unto a house of wine, and his banner over me is love." As mentioned earlier, wine represented the best pleasure the world could offer. Jesus' house of wine stands for the indescribable rich joys He will lavish on her.

This poor, sunburnt maiden must have felt unworthy in such a place. But he relieves her fear and bashfulness by waving over her a banner of His "love."

Like the maiden, we may often feel unworthy to be in Jesus' banquet hall enjoying all the rich blessings of His love. Yet, He says, it is My love that makes You worthy— the love I expressed when I shed my blood on the cross. "He who did not spare His own Son, but delivered Him up for us all, how shall He not with Him also freely give us all things?" (Romans 8:32 NKJV).

A banner announces that He will defend her. Under all circumstances, she can count on Him using all His resources to protect her.

We find our identity in being desired by God and in loving Him. Our worst enemy is often ourselves. We cannot believe that such generous love is intended for us. Others may perhaps be invited, but not us. But even if others make us feel of no value, He invites us to be under His banner of love. He longs for us to enjoy being loved, valued, and protected by Him,

Selah: Imagine living your life with the awareness that Jesus is constantly loving, valuing, and protecting you. How would believing these truths benefit you?

to persevere under trials & suffering
to remember even when treated poorly
by another that doesn't define me - Jesus defines me

2:5 Strengthen me with raisins, refresh me with apples, for I am faint with love.

The maiden is calling out for raisins and apples because they were refreshing. It is His Word that will sustain her! She needs the food of His Word. "When your words came, I ate them; they were my joy and my heart's delight" (Jeremiah 15:16).

She is overcome with delight because of the idea of being under His banner of love. He won her with His love and protects her with His love. Perhaps she was joyful to the point of exhaustion. Intense spiritual feeling can produce physical fatigue. She wanted Him to enlarge her capacity to be able to enjoy His glorious presence.

Selah: Jesus longs to refresh you. Sit in His Presence and read Psalm 23, 103, or 145. What promises encourage you?

1) The Lord is gracious & compassionate
Slow to anger & rich in love, Psalm 145:8
2. He redeems, heals, forgives Psalm 103
3. He is my faithful shepherd Psalm 23

2:6 His left arm is under my head, and his right arm embraces me.

She asked for His renewing love and He responded. Immediately she senses His tender, loving care for her. She feels secure and at rest as she realizes that "underneath are the everlasting arms" (Deuteronomy 33:37).

His left hand is under her head suggesting He is there to support her thoughts, to enable her to think His thoughts. "You will <u>keep in perfect peace</u> him whose mind is steadfast, because he trusts in you" (Isaiah 26:3).

The strength of His right hand embraces and draws her closer to His heart.

Selah: Write to Jesus asking to be in His embrace. Asking is an act of love and faith. It is allowing Him to have the inestimable joy of giving to you, His bride. Don't rob Him of that joy. The Lord Jesus Himself said, "It is more blessed to give than to receive" (Acts 20:35).

Dear Jesus. May I be held in your arms & protected in Your truth, love, life Always & in all ways,

2:7 Daughters of Jerusalem, I charge you by the gazelles and by the does of the field: Do not arouse or awaken love until it so desires.

A gazelle or doe has a sensitive nature and is easily startled. True love is a shy and gentle affection that can be easily disturbed. The bride is perfectly happy and such exquisite pleasure must not be bothered.

It is unclear who is giving the instructions to not disturb love, but perhaps because of a personal experience, I like to think it is the Holy Spirit. One Wednesday night on my way to attend a mid-week church service, I sensed a strong drawing to be alone with Jesus. I was early so slipped into the prayer room. Alone on my knees, I simply quietly enjoyed His presence. Soon I heard singing, and I began thinking that I should join the others. While trying to decide if I should leave the prayer room, I heard the Spirit say, "I want you to Myself."

Each of the three times in the Song of Songs (2:7; 3:7) these words "Do not arouse or awaken love until it so desires" are spoken, they are in the context of the Shulammite delighting in the presence of her Lover. We may be tempted to not linger in His presence but to get on with business as usual. There are times, though, that He wants us to Himself. The blessing of our union with Him is sweet communion. John Wesley commented on this verse, "Do not disturb nor offend Him."

If He leaves, the fault is always ours. Our less-than-enthusiastic affections may cause the same effect as when the multitude asked Jesus to depart: "So he got into the boat and left" (Luke 8:37).

Selah: Let's diligently seek to never quench the Spirit. Ask Jesus to draw you to Himself, and then take time to be alone with Him.

What are ways you can respond to His desire to be alone with you?

1. Make time, guard the time
2. Quiet my mind + listen
3. Let go of the "To-do" prayer list & just come to dwell in His Love

The Lover's Invitation

This is a new scene in the maiden's life with her Lover. She has learned to delight in Him, but Jesus yearns for her to join Him in His mission of sharing His love with others.

Beloved

2:8 Listen! My lover! Look! Here he comes, leaping across the mountains, bounding over the hills.
She now hears and sees Him coming toward her. He comes despite every obstacle. By leaping across the mountains, He is assuring her that no matter how intense the problems and difficulties may be, He has already conquered them.

He overcomes the hills of irritation, mental tiredness, physical weakness, busy schedules, and family difficulties. No obstacle can prevent us from enjoying sweet relationship with Christ if our hearts long for Him. "His divine power has given us everything we need for life and godliness" (1 Peter 1:3).

We may be like Mary and have a Martha who doesn't appreciate our sitting at Jesus' feet. Or our Martha may be our own voice within us telling we do not have time to "waste" at His feet or that we don't know how to spend time enjoying Him. But when we determine to seek Him, He will say to our Martha as He did to Mary's sister: "Mary has chosen what is better, and it will not be taken away from her" (Luke 10:42). He will overcome every difficulty when we seek to be near Him.

If we desire the inner joy that results from communion with Him and seek Him with all our heart, He will protect our schedules and will teach us how to draw near. He will skip over every hindrance Satan has designed to detract us from our love relationship with Jesus.

Selah: What things hinder you from spending regular time in His presence? Schedule, lack of desire...?

Focus on *Other people*

2:9 My lover is like a gazelle or a young stag. Look! There he stands behind our wall, gazing through the windows, peering through the lattice.

He is coming to invite her to arise and go with Him, but for the first time there is a wall between them. She now sees that she is not as close to Him as she once was. Even though He is her Lover, she has allowed something to separate them. Perhaps her faith has dwindled, her earnestness in prayer has decreased, or the Scriptures have been neglected.

He comes to us with great desire and He comes quickly like a gazelle because He is deeply in love with us.

Selah: Could there be a wall keeping you from sacred intimacy with Jesus? On a scale of 1 to 10, how sincere is your desire for Jesus' fellowship? *10*

① yes Conflicts w/my earthy Father

2:10 My lover spoke and said to me, "Arise, my darling, my beautiful one, and come with me."

He has answered her prayer to draw her, and she enjoys Him, but is it truly necessary to go on a mission with Him?

She has been resting under the apple tree and then in His embrace. Her enjoyment of Him pleases Him, but now He is asking her to arise and come with Him. She had thought He was simply for her personal pleasure. But He is about to tell her of His higher purpose for her—to live for His pleasure.

So when He says, "Arise!" He is asking her to do more than sit and enjoy His blessings. Would His beautiful darling be a partner with Him? He longs for lost and broken people to experience His love.

Selah: With words such as "my darling, my beautiful one," why do you think she hesitates? What kinds of things often hinder us from responding to Jesus when He challenges us to leave our comfort zone and do something for Him?

Fear on unknown
Fear of whether it is He who is really calling
Fear of rejection, failure

2:11 See! The winter is past; the rains are over and gone.

2:12 Flowers appear on the earth; the season of singing has come, the cooing of doves is heard in our land.

2:13 The fig tree forms its early fruit; the blossoming vines spread their fragrance. Arise, come, my darling; my beautiful one, come with me.

To encourage her to trust Him, He reminds her of the transformation that has taken place in her since that first cry of her heart. The dark times in her life are past. The springtime has come; it's the time of singing. The earth is blossoming again and flowers appear on the earth. This is a picture of what takes place in the heart of one who falls in love with Jesus. The cold winter of loneliness, misery, and selfishness is past, and the time of singing has come.

He tells her that the season of harvest is close. The voice of the dove is heard in Israel when it is time to gather crops. Green figs appear just before the mature figs. The fragrance of the young grapes indicates the harvest is near. He is continuing to answer her prayer to draw her to Himself by inviting her to join Him in the vineyard. He speaks tenderly and repeats, "Arise, come, my darling; my beautiful one, come with me." Surely she will be motivated to obey Him when she has such assurances of how loved and beautiful she is in His eyes.

Selah: The maiden had ears to hear His call to arise and come with Him after her time of resting in His arms. How are you to know when the Lord calls you to arise and follow? Have you begun to see a need that you had not noticed before or repeatedly had an idea of something you could do for Him? *Be in the*

Be a beacon of prayer

Be a resident force of prayer wherever I go

Lover *Write a book "my walk w/ Jesus — a Love story"*

2:14 My dove in the clefts of the rock, in the hiding places on the mountainside, show me your face, let me hear your voice; for your voice is sweet, and your face is lovely.

Her Lover reveals His tender affection for her as He calls her "My dove." A dove is gentle and faithful. The dove hides on the mountainside rather than seeking to be noticed. He admired her for avoiding all needless attention to herself.

For her to want to arise and come with Him she must be in close communion with Him, so He asks to hear her adoring worship and her prayer. This is an <u>invitation</u> for <u>her to intercede</u> and <u>cry out to Him</u>. He is telling her, "You have focused on your satisfaction and what I am to you. Now <u>let me take pleasure in you</u>."

Listen to the tone of His voice. He doesn't brow beat her but encourages her. He comes as One who yearns for her fellowship. He does not remind her of all she previously said concerning Him—how He was her bundle of myrrh, her delight, the special tree among all other trees. It is amazing that the Sovereign One deals with His loved one in pleading tones. He says, "Let me hear..."

Jesus finds delight in His times of fellowship with us. He says, "I enjoy you. I call you delightful and I love you! Give Me your worship, for it is sweet." Jesus calls your prayer life sweet!

Selah: He desires close communion with you—He stoops to see and hear when you look into His face and speak to Him! Will you praise Jesus, either with your outer or your inner voice (silent whispers of your heart)? It is fragrant incense to Him.

Take a few moments to whisper words of praise using the alphabet. "God, You are Amazing, Beloved, Creator...." See Appendix C.

Or "Sing to him a new song" (Psalm 33:3). Use new words and melody to praise Him.

2:15 Catch for us the foxes, the little foxes that ruin the vineyards, our vineyards that are in bloom.

Before she can go with Him, though, there is something she must do. She must get rid of those little foxes that caused a wall between them. Foxes are cunning animals that will destroy a vineyard during the night. Our vineyard refers to our fellowship or connection with God that produces fruit. Foxes destroy fruitfulness.

He is addressing the subtle areas that seem so minor, yet capable of wounding our love for Him. Foxes are known for their crafty, devious natures, so we use the expression "sly as a fox." The difficulty is that when foxes are little they appear so innocent. But little foxes, if not destroyed, grow up to be big foxes. We get used to them when they are small, and we fail to notice they damage our relationship with Jesus.

What are some of the little foxes that will ruin our spiritual vineyards? Susanna Wesley wrote to her son John:

"Take this rule: whatever ...impairs the tenderness of your conscience...or takes off your relish of spiritual things... that thing is sin to you, however innocent it may be in itself."

Jesus is very sensitive to anything that makes Him feel second-place. A friend had prayed fervently for God to answer his prayer, but it seemed God was not listening. One day God spoke clearly. "The hindrance is the idol in your life." He had no idea that he had an idol. "Your idol is playing games on the internet." A little fox takes our time and attention away from Him.

Is something other than your time with Jesus your priority for your day? Is there unforgiveness buried deep in your heart over something that may have happened years ago? Does the Spirit have access to your money, both to limit your spending and to prompt you to give? Are you excusing a critical, complaining, or impatient spirit—any unChristlike attitude? Is there a secret sin in your thought life or in what you look at on the internet? Too much secular reading or hours watching TV or a lustful habit all grieve the Holy Spirit and threaten to ruin the whole vineyard unless dealt with.

One day Jesus showed me a little fox in my vineyard. He gave me the sad feeling it gave Him. He was jealous of that "little fox." "...the LORD, whose name is Jealous, is a jealous God" (Exodus 34:14).

Jesus says, "Catch for us;" it is a joint project. He will help us and show us where the foxes hide when we pray, "Search me, O God, and know my heart" (Psalm 139:23). He does not bring the little fox to our minds if He does not have plans to destroy it. He can always enable us to be rid of anything that hinders us from enjoying intimacy with Him.

Selah: Is there a little fox robbing you of intimacy with Jesus? Right now confess it, determine to forsake, and trust Jesus to forgive and restore you. "Test me, O Lord, and try me, examine my heart and my mind; for your love is ever before me" (Psalm 26:2-3).

"Have mercy on me, O God, have mercy on me, for in you my soul takes refuge. I will take refuge in the shadow of your wings" (Psalm 57:1).

The Consequences of Little Foxes

Being with Jesus was delightful! But would the maiden get rid of the "little foxes" and follow Him?

Beloved

2:16 My lover is mine and I am his; he browses among the lilies.
He is hers! He is hers to lean upon, to bear all her burdens, to provide all her needs, to enjoy. What a glorious realization! She is sincerely enjoying this magnificent truth but she lacks maturity. She mentions herself first. He is her lover. The focus is on the fact that their relationship is only for her enjoyment. She sees no danger, and there's a hint of self-centeredness in her words, "My beloved is mine."

It seems she thinks she has a secure position and doesn't need to be concerned about the little foxes. It is as though she is saying, "He is mine and I am His and nothing can alter that relationship. I can find Him at any time; He feeds His flock among the lilies."

Notice she did not obey the Lord's request in 2:14, "Let me see your face and hear your voice." She is less interested in what pleases Him than in what pleases her. She fails the first test of practical surrender although there is no question that she loves Him.

In Hosea 14:5, the prophet calls God's people a lily, so when He was browsing among the lilies, He was enjoying His people. Jesus delights to dwell and be nourished in His heart with the praises of His people. She would find His presence when she worshiped with them.

When I'm with a group of other believers, I love to think of Jesus browsing among the lilies. He is delighting in our fellowship.

Selah: What are the first words that come to mind when you think of your devotional life? *Love*

How might it benefit your daily time with Jesus if you thought of it as your response to His words, "Let me see your face and hear your voice"?

2:17 Until the day breaks and the shadows flee, turn, my lover, and be like a gazelle or like a young stag on the rugged hills.

With sadness she acknowledges that Jesus must go and be like the gazelle of 2:9. There are areas of her life that are not fully in the light, so she says that until the day breaks and the shadows in her life flee, He must turn and go. She lightly dismisses Him with the thought, *A little later I will go with Him.* Refusing to destroy little foxes resulted in hardness of her heart. The grieved Bridegroom departs.

The words "rugged hills" are sometimes translated "the hills of Bether." Bether means separation or division. She wants Him to stay with her, but she is not ready to get

45

rid of the little foxes, the shadows in her life that separate them.

Isn't it amazing that she is asking the Lord to turn? It is as if she is saying, "I know what is best for us. You need to turn and change Your mind about my little fox. These shadows are but a small thing."

Christians often want to have the fullness of Jesus' Spirit in their lives plus compromising sin. We can't walk with the Lord and have sin continue in our lives once He has made us aware of what displeases Him.

Even though she had begun to walk the surrendered life, she had things buried deep within her heart that needed to be dealt with. Why didn't He make her go with Him? If he had coerced her, the little fox of selfishness would still remain. Although hidden for a while, it would rise again in another circumstance.

The Lord will allow her to see all the ugliness and damage caused by a little bit of her will mixed into the surrendered life. This decision to not go with Him unreservedly will cost her dearly.

In the solemn night she discovered her mistake. It was dark, and she was alone. Retiring to rest, she still hoped for His return.

Selah: Notice how easily she chose to not respond to Jesus. Why is it often easy for us to ignore the still, small voice that warns about a "little fox"?

3:1 All night long on my bed I looked for the one my heart loves; I looked for him but did not find him.

One moment of willful, deliberate selfishness cost her dearly. The trap set by the enemy caught her. The joy, peace and contentment of chapters one and two have fled.

Now she is on her bed hoping to find rest; it used to be their bed. Their partnership was disrupted. Still she is sincere when she calls Him the One she loves.

It is night when He is gone. On her bed she searched her heart to see how she had offended him. She finds out those little foxes were really a trick of the enemy. What she thought she needed turned out to bring separation from the One who alone truly satisfied her.

For her good and her restoration, she is experiencing Hebrews 12:6: "The Lord disciplines those he loves, and he punishes everyone he accepts as a son." Godly sorrow has come and is doing an amazing work in her. Now she understands what it cost her to not fully obey. We often think of the cost to obey but conveniently forget the enormous cost of disobedience.

Selah: Consider what the cost of failing to get rid of your "little fox" might cost you. *intimacy & Freedom in Christ*

3:2 I will get up now and go about the city, through its streets and squares; I will search for the one my heart loves. So I looked for him but did not find him.

The pain of losing His presence motivates her to arise off her bed and leave the comfort zone. Perhaps she seeks Him through the spiritual disciplines of prayer and meditation on the Word as she did in the past. But prayer and fasting are no substitute for obedience. Now it appears that she is willing to pay the price of getting rid of what keeps her from His presence. No more will the little foxes spoil her vineyard.

Why did she not find Him? She wanted Him in her own way, her own time. She needed to learn that His invitation to come with Him was not to be taken lightly.

47

Once we ignore His call to obey Him or His prompting to pray, we may try later but find that to do what He asked without His help is either impossible or unfruitful.

We should allow God to search our hearts and put His finger on any hindrance. Is there someone who hurt you long ago who needs your forgiveness? Is there a wrong attitude that Jesus does not approve? This humbling time seems difficult. "No discipline seems pleasant at the time, but painful" (Hebrews 12:11). Later on, however, it produces a harvest of righteousness and brings refreshing peace.

Selah: When God seems distant, what should we do? See Isaiah 59:20, Ezekiel 14:6, and Acts 3:19.

The redeemer will come to Zion, to those in Jacob who repent of their sin. Isaiah 59:20
... Repent! Then turn from your idols & renounce all your detestable practices. Ezekiel 14:6

3:3 The watchmen found me as they made their rounds in the city. "Have you seen the one my heart loves?"

The maiden still loved Him even though she had not responded quickly to His invitation. She is seeking Him with her whole heart. She does not care who in the city knows, as long as she finds Him. She will confess to others that He has withdrawn Himself from her; she will speak to the watchmen—those who are to watch over her soul—and ask them if they can help her. She must be honest. What matters is not what people think of her! She must find Him! He promises, "You will seek me and find me when you seek me with all your heart...I will be found by you" (Jeremiah 29:13).

She had humbled herself by letting her overseers know she had lost Him. Jesus quickly responded to her humility and earnestness.

Selah: Is the Spirit leading you to humble yourself by letting others know you need spiritual help and asking them to pray for you?

Repent, then & turn to God, so that your sins may be wiped out, that times of refreshing may come from the Lord, & that He may send the Messiah, who has been appointed for you - even Jesus. Acts 3:19

When you confess and forsake your sins and failures,
how does that help both you and others?

Sets me Free + encourages others (hopefully)

**3:4 Scarcely had I passed them when I found the one my heart
loves. I held him and would not let him go till I had brought him
to my mother's house, to the room of the one who conceived
me.**

She had told others of her heart's longing, had spoken
of her love for Him, and He could not resist coming to her.
She said she would not let Him go, but Christ is not eager
to leave us. It is always we who let Him go.

Her "mother's house" refers to those who brought her
to Jesus. She now wanted to share her joy with those who
had helped her find Him.

Jesus told of a woman who searched diligently for her
lost silver coin: "And when she finds it, she calls her
friends and neighbors together and says, 'Rejoice with me;
I have found my lost coin'" (Luke 15:9).

Selah: Take a moment to write a prayer of
thanksgiving for the one who helped you turn to Jesus.
Email your prayer to that person if possible.

Carla Bergen from BSF
Giti Hansen from ST Augustine's } through bible study

**3:5 Daughters of Jerusalem, I charge you by the gazelles and by
the does of the field: Do not arouse or awaken love until it so
desires.**

Once again she is delighting in Him. The Holy Spirit
very gently reminds her to continue to enjoy His
communion as long as she likes.

"My soul will be satisfied as with the richest of foods;
with singing lips my mouth will praise you. On my bed I

remember you; I think of you through the watches of the night" (Psalm 63:5-6).

Selah: Write a list of at least 50 loving things Jesus has done for you. Take time to praise Him and to receive His love.

1. He revealed Himself to me
2. He waited patiently for me
3. He "wooed" me
4. He forgave me
5. He saved me
6. He teaches me
7. He is loving to me
8. He hears my cry
9. He comforts me
10. He protects me
11. He guides me
12. He talks to me
13. He holds me
14. He corrects me
15. He prunes me
16. He Helps me
17. He sees me
18. He shares His pain with me as I share mine with Him
19. He helps me to love what He loves
20. He helps me to hate what He hats
21. He teaches me about compassion
22. He teaches me about grace
23. He brings me great joy
24. He brings me great comfort
25. He joins me in great sorrow
26. He never forsakes me
27. He walks with me
28. He gives me breath
29. He Hides me under His banner
30. He validates my worth to Him

50

The Celebration

When we receive Jesus' love, we have great joy, but His joy knows no bounds. There is a celebration in Heaven beyond all we can imagine when we give ourselves to Him.

Friends

3:6 Who is this coming up from the desert like a column of smoke, perfumed with myrrh and incense made from all the spices of the merchant?

In the phrase "Who is this" the Hebrew word for "this" is feminine, so we know it refers to the maiden. She had destroyed the foxes that were spoiling her vineyard and had sought her Lord until she found Him. Now she is ready to leave the desert (wilderness) life, and her Lover celebrates.

The daughters of Jerusalem recognize it is a bridal procession. The King is bringing in His bride with royal honors! Smoke is the result of the fire of the Holy Spirit.

His extravagant expenditures of spices and fragrance tell us He spared nothing. He is bringing her out of the desert, the wilderness of unbelief, into union with Himself, and He is celebrating with great joy.

Selah: Zephaniah wrote, "The Lord your God is with you....He will take great delight in you...He will rejoice over you with singing" (3:17).

What is your response to this thought: "When I fully give myself to Jesus, He celebrates with great joy and singing"? *That it is utter foolishness to hold back*

3:7 Look! It is Solomon's carriage, escorted by sixty warriors, the noblest of Israel,

3:8 all of them wearing the sword, all experienced in battle, each with his sword at his side, prepared for the terrors of the night.

The warriors are noble because they fight the battles. They are the prayer warriors who escort the carriage! Without them, there would not be this union between the Bride and the Bridegroom.

Intercessors are like warriors. They come bringing their sword, the Word. They have fought many battles on their knees, and they are self-controlled, alert, and aware of the enemy. "Be self-controlled and alert. Your enemy the devil prowls around like a roaring lion looking for someone to devour" (1 Peter 5:8).

A friend received a sad phone call and was possibly facing estrangement from her son. That day someone emailed her, "Why did God wake me up at 3 a.m. today to pray for you?" Then my friend knew why she had been able to cast her burden on the Lord and trust Him to give her wisdom for the situation.

Selah: Do you recall a time when someone else's prayers helped you to be an overcomer? *yes - Raymond when I couldn't fight the enemy of oppression Rel: F.V. alone*

Who do you think depends upon your intercessions? *My family & friends*

3:9 King Solomon made for himself the carriage; he made it of wood from Lebanon.

3:10 Its posts he made of silver, its base of gold. Its seat was upholstered with purple, its interior lovingly inlaid by the daughters of Jerusalem.

Jesus spoke into existence the tree that was fashioned into His cross. By His death on Calvary, He constructed a way to express His love to the entire world. Wood from Lebanon was the most costly and fragrant wood. His sacrifice on the cross was both expensive and sweet smelling.

The King added posts of silver and a base of gold. The pillars of silver symbolize redemption He provided at Calvary, and the "gold" speaks of the divine life—her indwelling Lord. The upholstery of purple points to the royalty of the Lord Jesus.

The daughters of Jerusalem speak of His people who participate in the necessary nurturing and supporting.

3:11 Come out, you daughters of Zion, and look at King Solomon wearing the crown, the crown with which his mother crowned him on the day of his wedding, the day his heart rejoiced.

The king wears a crown that His mother gave Him. Matthew 12:50 tells us who His mother is. "For whoever does the will of my Father in heaven is my brother and sister and mother." He considers us intimate family because of our unreserved willingness to do His will.

"Come...look at King Solomon." Early in our relationship with Jesus, we may want others to notice our gifts, our ministry, our successes. But when we have fully given ourselves to Jesus, our fleshly ambition for personal recognition and prominence no longer motivates us.

We underestimate the joy our union with Jesus brings Him. This wedding day—the day we give ourselves to Him completely—is called the day of His gladness. We recognize that when we fully surrender we have unspeakable joy, but our joy pales in comparison to the joy our union gives Jesus. He has longed to be one with us.

Selah: "The day his heart rejoiced" refers to the day you became His bride, the day you became united to Him. When did you give Jesus this joy? If you haven't, why not now?

Many times - each seemingly at a deeper, fuller level.
The day I accepted Him as my Lord & Savior I was His - but I didn't have a personal relationship w/ Him until I started studying Scripture.

What Jesus Admires

In this section the Bridegroom declares His love for His bride by telling her what He admires. She had asked for His kisses which He gives through the words that come from His mouth. As she listens to Him, she matures spiritually.

We, too, grow spiritually by receiving His love through His words. As we daily receive His "kisses" through reading and reflecting on Scripture, we gain these qualities Jesus admires.

Lover

4:1 How beautiful you are, my darling! Oh, how beautiful!

Song of Songs is an amazing revelation of what our Beloved sees in us who have fully surrendered everything to Him for His pleasure and His use. Too often we see ourselves as undesirable. That is why this book is so important. He wants us to hear Him say, "How beautiful you are, my darling! Oh, how beautiful!" He says it twice.

Why? Because we find it so difficult to believe that Jesus sees us as truly lovely.

Jesus told Peter that he would deny Him (John 13:36-38). Yet in the very next breath, Jesus said, "Do not let your heart be troubled...."

Jesus knew Peter's deep love for Him would immediately cause him to weep bitterly. (Matthew 26:75) A truly surrendered believer responds to sin in the same way. An unsurrendered believer is hardened to his sin and does not repent.

As we read the Word, we will hear again and again that He treasures and admires us. Six times in Scripture He calls us His "treasured possession." (See Exodus 19:5, Deuteronomy 7:6, 14:2, 26:18, Psalm 135:4 and Malachi 3:17.) The Hebrew word is *segullah* and is a jeweler's term describing an object of great beauty and value that brings exquisite delight.

Selah: Why do we have difficulty believing that Jesus sees us as beautiful and that we bring Him delight?

Because of our sinful flesh. It is so easy to focus on what is wrong w/ us (unsurrendered) life vs. what is right - God in us

Your eyes behind your veil are doves. Your hair is like a flock of goats descending from Mount Gilead.

4:2 Your teeth are like a flock of sheep just shorn, coming up from the washing. Each has its twin; not one of them is alone.

He first mentions her eyes. Jesus looks behind the veil and sees that all she truly wants is to allow His Spirit to live within her. He had mentioned earlier that she had dove's eyes. He mentions them again because her ability to focus on Him has increased. Our ability to keep our eyes on Jesus also increases as we read His Word.

Hair is a symbol of consecration to God. A Nazarite was forbidden to cut his hair as a sign of his dedication to

God. Samson had supernatural strength only if his hair remained long.

Goats are used in the Bible as sin offerings. Her Bridegroom says her giving herself totally to Him is as though she has offered Him a whole flock of goats.

Without teeth we are limited in what we can eat. Paul spoke of the immature who could not eat solid food so he could only give them milk. (1 Corinthians 3:1-3) She is capable of eating the strong meat of the Word. (Hebrews 5:13-14) Christ is pleased when we can take in and enjoy the rich truths He gives us.

She loves His Word and spiritually feasts upon it. Why? Because her Lover shares secrets through His Word. She could say with Jeremiah, "When your words came, I ate them; they were my joy and my heart's delight," (Jeremiah 15:16).

Because she takes in the Word, she is washed. (John 15:3) "Christ loved the church and gave himself up for her to make her holy, cleansing her by the washing with water through the word" (Ephesians 5:25, 26).

"Each has its twin." She is balanced and does not reject some things and receive other things.

Selah: How would you describe the difference between merely reading the Word and feasting on it?

Applying it - making it personal Claiming it as my truth to live by

4:3 Your lips are like a scarlet ribbon; your mouth is lovely.

With her teeth she took in food, and with her lips she expresses what she has received from the Word. Scarlet speaks of redemption. Just as the scarlet cord in Joshua 2:21 provided redemption for Rahab and her family, so the Bride's words are redemptive and bless others.

She knows instinctively in His presence some words and comments are not appropriate for one in union with Him. "Nor should there be obscenity, foolish talk or coarse joking, which are out of place, but rather thanksgiving" (Ephesians 5:4).

He will delight in our wholesome speech when we meditate and are careful to obey Ephesians 4:29: "Don't use foul or abusive language. Let everything you say be good and helpful, so that your words will be an encouragement to those who hear them" (Ephesians 4:29 NLT).

Selah: How does regularly meditating on Scripture affect our speech? *It magnifies the harsh ugliness of vulgarity*

Your temples behind your veil are like the halves of a pomegranate.

The temple represents the place of our thinking processes. Hers is covered with a veil indicating it is hidden from view. What part of our thinking processes is hidden from others' view but not from God's? Our motives. He sees behind what we say and do, the reasons we make our choices. "You alone know the hearts of men" (2 Chronicles 6:30).

The red of the pomegranate represents the blood of Jesus. Because of His blood, she has the ability to make her choices—not according to what impresses others but according to what pleases Him.

The skin of the pomegranate hides its beautiful interior. Our life in Christ is characterized by a kind and courteous spirit—not from hidden impure motives, but by a true grace that flows from Him who dwells within.

For us to keep our motives pure, it is important that everything that enters our minds be filtered through what He would approve—every TV, video and radio program, every magazine and book and all we view on the Internet.

Selah: How careful do you think most Christians are to guard against having wrong motives? See 1 Chronicles 28:9.

4:4 Your neck is like the tower of David, built with elegance; on it hang a thousand shields, all of them shields of warriors.

4:5 Your two breasts are like two fawns, like twin fawns of a gazelle that browse among the lilies.

The neck signifies the will in Scripture. "I knew how stubborn you were; the sinews of your neck were iron" (Isaiah 48:4). Those stubborn and proud of heart are called stiff-necked. "They did not listen to me or pay attention. They were stiff-necked" (Jeremiah 7:26).

To Jesus, the maiden's neck was beautiful. It was strong like a tower. She is resolute; she will do His will. "I have set my face like a stone, determined to do his will." (Isaiah 50:7).

Because of her determination in prayer, she is a mighty prayer warrior.

1 Thessalonians 5:8 tells us to put on the breastplate of faith and love, so the two breasts symbolize these virtues. She has fed on Him, the living Word and now can provide food for others. It is our faith and love that nourish others. "The only thing that counts is faith expressing itself through love" (Galatians 5:6). He assures her that she has both.

Selah: Why are both faith and love needed as we nourish others? _to keep pure motives_

Beloved

4:6 Until the day breaks and the shadows flee, I will go to the mountain of myrrh and to the hill of incense.

She responds to His loving admiration with a greater desire to allow nothing between them. In 1:13 she recognized that to follow Him would mean sacrifice, and now she promises to go to the mountain of myrrh and submit to Him. She will go to the hill of incense and give herself to intercession and worship.

In 2:17 she had told him, "Until the day breaks and the shadows flee, turn, my lover, and be like a gazelle or like a young stag on the rugged hills." She had asked Him to turn and go without her. He had left, and she learned she could not live without His presence.

She realizes, though, that she is still living with some shadows in her life. The closer we come to Christ, the more obvious our imperfections are to us. She is determined to be rid of anything hindering her relationship with Him.

Selah: "You will know the truth, and the truth will set you free" (John 8:32). Have there been shadows (sins, bondages) in your life that the Word has helped you overcome? If so, what Scripture gave you freedom?

Jesus Finds No Flaw

The maiden's promise to go to the mountain of myrrh, the place of full surrender, moves the heart of Jesus. He sees beauty in her because she has taken steps to live out her obedience. He knows her "yes" is sincere.

Lover

4:7 All beautiful you are, my darling; there is no flaw in you.

He says there is no flaw in her. Just admitting there are shadows in her life makes her perfect in His sight. That is our God—always looking beyond our faults and judging us by our good intentions and deep desires. He delights in seeing the good in us, and He admires us even in our weakest moments far more than we can comprehend.

Someone had offended my friend, and for three days she could not get past her irritation. She said, "I didn't feel like talking to God or even hearing from Him. I was miserable feeling that way, but that is how it was. I was driving home from work when suddenly I looked at the license plate on the car in front of me. It said my name and then 4511. As soon as I got home, I looked up Psalm 45:11 and read, 'The king is enthralled by your beauty.' My heart melted before Him."

How like Jesus to send a message of love when she felt unworthy! When we think He is far away, He is only around the corner with arms wide open. Knowing He loves us changes us.

Selah: Are you looking for perfection in yourself? Jesus is looking for a total surrender of your will to His. He will give you time to grow into His likeness. He delights in you even when you are weak. How would fully believing this concept change you?

4:8 Come with me from Lebanon, my bride, come with me from Lebanon. Descend from the crest of Amana, from the top of Senir, the summit of Hermon, from the lions' dens and the mountain haunts of the leopards.

She agreed to go in 4:6, so once again He invites her to come with Him. It is in connection with this loving invitation that He changes the word my "love" for the more endearing term, my "bride." Her willingness to be abandoned to Him and her commitment to come into intimate partnership with Him has ravished His heart. He will reveal to her what God wants to do among the people of the earth and teach her to engage in spiritual warfare against the "lions" and "leopards."

"Come with me." That is always His invitation. When Jesus said, "Go and make disciples of all nations," He preceded it with, "All authority in heaven and on earth has been given to me," and followed it with "Surely I am with you always" (Matthew 28:18-20). He goes with us when we purpose to make disciples whether we're in our own neighborhood or in a foreign country.

Lebanon was a beautiful country bordering Israel but it was also a compromising nation. He is calling her to flee all temptations to compromise as she goes with Him.

4:9 You have stolen my heart, my sister, my bride; you have stolen my heart with one glance of your eyes, with one jewel of your necklace.

This verse summarizes the Song of Songs. I like the King James version: "Thou hast ravished my heart, my sister, [my] spouse; thou hast ravished my heart with one of thine eyes." To be "ravished" can be defined as "to be filled with emotions of joy and delight because of one who is unusually attractive."

He is more than a Bridegroom to her. "Anyone who does the will of my Father in heaven is my brother and sister and mother!" (Matthew 12:50). He delights in every relationship He has with us.

Her acceptance of His invitation to go with Him to seek and to rescue the perishing has ravished His heart. How incredible that we are able to delight His heart by simply saying "Yes" to Him. Our passionate Bridegroom cherishes us and sees us as beautiful each time we desire to do any small thing for Him.

Another translation says, "You have captured my heart" (NLT). One glance from our eyes does to Him what the armies and kings cannot do—we conquer Him fully. We steal His heart with just one loving thought, one heartfelt thank you, one loving act we do thinking, "This is just for You, Jesus!" Each look of devotion, every prayer, each whisper of love moves His heart.

The necklace speaks of her submitted will. He looked into her eyes and saw her willingness to answer to any demands He would make. Our submission is His greatest pleasure.

Jesus proclaims two times that we ravish His heart because He is so eager for us to believe it. The more we understand God's affections for us, the more passion for God we will have.

For the first time He calls her "my sister." In Luke 8:21, He said his immediate family includes those who hear God's Word and obey it. She was eager to observe carefully all He was asking her to do.

She proudly displays the chain around her neck so that all might know to Whom she belongs. She is not embarrassed to display the chain of surrender and the crucified life to others. This thrills His heart.

Selah: What does this verse teach about Jesus' affections for you?

4:10 How delightful is your love, my sister, my bride! How much more pleasing is your love than wine, and the fragrance of your perfume than any spice!

We may think that our love is too faint, but whatever we possess is very sweet to Jesus. When we come to Him we not only receive but we also give Him joy beyond our comprehension. Our adoration brings refreshment to His heart. Even our small expressions of love to Him are delightful.

The glory of the stars and galaxies surely must bring Jesus pleasure. Yet even all of His beautiful creation is not enough to meet His heart's need for love. It is His dear surrendered believers whose love and passion satisfy Him.

At the beginning of the story she said His love is better than wine. Now He makes that same comment about her love. Her love satisfies Him.

The word "perfume" means oil in the Hebrew. The reference to her oils refers to the release of the Spirit in the life of the believer. She has spent so much time with Him that she now has the same fragrance as He—the aroma of Christ (2 Corinthians 2:15).

This great fragrance comes through the brokenness in her life. Gethsemane means "oil press." When we go through our Gethsemane fully surrendered, a sweet fragrance is released from our lives.

A godly minister had an only child who was at the point of death. When the doctor informed these parents there was no hope their son would live, in their anguish they cried out that God was unkind.

Then the Holy Spirit reminded them that God is love and gave them grace to accept whatever God allowed. The father said, "We must not let God *take* our child. We must *give* him." So kneeling at the bedside, they humbly gave back to God the child He had loaned them for a short time.

The fragrance of Christ came into their lives in a fresh way. Every person in their congregation sensed a wonderfully sweet spirit in this fully surrendered couple.

Selah: Why is the depth of our love for Jesus expressed most accurately during difficult times? *Because that is when I am most vulnerable, open + connected to Jesus, my dependence is totally on Him alone.*

4:11 Your lips drop sweetness as the honeycomb, my bride; milk and honey are under your tongue. The fragrance of your garments is like that of Lebanon.

Her lips refer to her speech. He hears every word she says. As she seeks the lost, loves the needy, and witnesses of Him to others, the words of her lips are as sweet as honey. Honey restores the weak ones, and milk feeds the immature ones. She gives to each just the right words.

Milk represents the Word of God. "Like newborn babies, crave pure spiritual milk, so that by it you may grow up in your salvation" (1 Peter 2:2). The delights of the Word of God are compared to honey dripping from the honeycomb. "They are more precious than gold, than much pure gold; they are sweeter than honey, than honey from the comb" (Psalm 19:10).

Her lips bring Him great happiness. In 1:2 she yearned for Him to kiss her with the kisses of His mouth, with precious revelation from His Word. She gives back what He had given to her.

Garments speak of outward conduct—her activities, entertainment, and conversation. Even though she lives in the world, she has His fragrance because she has spent so much time with Him. Paul mentions the fragrance of the sweet aroma of Christ that comes from the redeemed:

"But thanks be to God, who always leads us in triumphal procession in Christ and through us spreads everywhere the fragrance of the knowledge of him. For we are to God the aroma of Christ among those who are being saved and those who are perishing. To the one we are the smell of death; to the other, the fragrance of life" (2 Corinthians 2:14-16).

Every loving deed done humbly for Jesus, no matter how insignificant, will not go unnoticed by the King. Through such deeds, we carry His sweet aroma.

Selah: Have you ever been with a believer who seemed to exude a special spiritual influence over you that you could not find words to describe? That is the fragrance of a life lived in loving submission to the Holy Spirit. What qualities attracted you to that person?

Peace, light

66

Christ in You

Not only in the words you say,
Not only in your deeds confessed,
But in the most unconscious way
Is Christ confessed.

Is it a beautiful smile,
A holy light upon your brow?
Oh no! I felt His presence
When you laughed, just now.

For me 'twas not the truth you taught
(To you so clear, to me so dim)
But when you came to me, you brought
A sense of Him.

And from your eyes He beckons me,
And from your lips His love is shed
Till I lose sight of you, and see
The Christ instead.
—Anonymous

Our Turning Point

The maiden's time of listening to Jesus has changed her. Her heart now belongs totally to Jesus, and she discovers she desires to work for Him. Activities done only for self-fulfillment no longer satisfy.

4:12 You are a garden locked up, my sister, my bride; you are a spring enclosed, a sealed fountain.

The garden of her heart is beautiful because of her absolute surrender of her will. Now her heart is only for Him! She is sealed from all others and lives exclusively for His pleasure. This is holiness—to live for Him and Him alone. She has given Him full, loving control. She seeks to read, watch, say, and listen to what she knows would please Him.

Our minds are to be kept locked so that our imaginations and fantasies are kept pure. When we lock out the enemy, our secret thoughts, meditations, and ambitions are like cool streams of water to Jesus.

If you have difficulty keeping your thought life pure, cleanse yourself through His Word. Ask the Holy Spirit to give you a promise. Then apply that Word to the problem by faith. If we allow Him, He "is able to keep [us] from falling and to present [us] before his glorious presence without fault and with great joy" (Jude 24). Claim 1 Corinthians 10:13. *No temptation has seized you except what is common to man...*

Selah: The Psalmist promised, "I will refuse to look at anything vile and vulgar" (Psalm 101:3 NLT). What is a practical application of that verse for you?
Not dwelling on how my Father speaks & treats me & my loved ones

According to Psalm 119:9, how can we cleanse ourselves from what displeases Jesus?
Live according to His word

4:13 Your plants are an orchard of pomegranates with choice fruits, with henna and nard,

4:14 nard and saffron, calamus and cinnamon, with every kind of incense tree, with myrrh and aloes and all the finest spices.

4:15 You are a garden fountain, a well of flowing water streaming down from Lebanon.

She has now moved beyond a quest for what God can do for her to an understanding that God wishes to produce fruit in her life.

Her heart is an orchard of pomegranates with other precious plants growing among them! She is filled with love for the blood of Jesus (represented by the red of the pomegranates). He has chosen and appointed her to bear fruit (John 15:16), and He sees the fruit of the Spirit in her (Galatians 5:22). His Father is glorified where there is much fruit (John 15:8), for others will say, "This land that was laid waste has become like the garden of Eden" (Ezekiel 36:37).

He sees a great variety in her that He admires. She gives forth the fragrance of a life filled with praise to God. What God seeks in our lives is not external performance or an impressive record of achievements but the fruit of the Spirit. *Gal. 5:22 Love, joy, peace, patience, kindness, goodness, faithfulness, gentleness & self-control*

He compares the wisdom that flows from her to the rivers flowing out of Lebanon that are crystal clear. Her heart is the temple of the Holy Spirit, and the wisdom and graces that flow from her are pure.

The water is streaming down—so it flows without effort. When we are filled with His Spirit, we refresh others without human effort.

Selah: "Those who remain in me, and I in them, will produce much fruit. For apart from me you can do nothing" (John 15:5). Notice that we produce much fruit by remaining in Him. What does does it mean to "remain" in Him? *Be in obedience, submission & gratitude to God the Father, Jesus, the Son & the Holy Spirit.*

Beloved

4:16 Awake, north wind, and come, south wind! Blow on my garden, that its fragrance may spread abroad. Let my lover come into his garden and taste its choice fruits.

The maiden, moved by His loving words, tells Him, "Come what may—the north winds of adversity or the south winds of blessings—may the fragrance of my love for You spread abroad." She will love Him no matter what He brings so that the fragrance of her love for Him will be obvious to others.

She is saying, "Lord, whatever it is that is getting in the way of my love growing and maturing, move it out of the way." Also, she is transitioning from "my garden" to "His garden." She sees her life and ministry as His garden instead of hers. In the heart that is totally God's, there comes a desire to work for Him.

This is a turning point. Before she loved him for her personal enjoyment. She had said, "Like an apple tree among the trees of the forest is my lover among the young men. I delight to sit in his shade."

Now she says, "Let Him come to His garden so He can enjoy its pleasant fruits." She is not content just to enjoy Him for her own pleasure. She is saying, "Please let my garden yield fruit for You—fruit that others will enjoy." She prays that the winds would allow the presence of God to flow out of her life in a way that was evident to others.

When we begin to do our activities out of love for Jesus, the reward will be grace to love Him more. We no longer need a list of do's and don'ts when we have a hunger to show Him our love in all we do.

"Deep calls to deep" (Psalm 42:7). God created a "deep" within each of us that is capable of responding to this "deep" call from Him. The "deep" within us is a "garden" in which we commune and fellowship with God. Jesus said we are to go into our closet and shut the door (Matthew 6:6). Think of this not as a physical space but a special place within where we turn aside to commune with Him. "Come, my lover, let us go to the countryside...there I will give you my love" (Song of Songs 7:11, 12).

Selah: Do you do things for Jesus out of a sense of duty or because of your love for Him?

How will others be affected if our love for Jesus is our motivation? *It will be an inspirational attraction*

71

5:1 I have come into my garden, my sister, my bride; I have gathered my myrrh with my spice. I have eaten my honeycomb and my honey; I have drunk my wine and my milk.

Friends

Eat, O friends, and drink; drink your fill, O lovers.

In the previous verse she invited Him to come into His garden and taste its choice fruits. He responds, "Yes!" and comes immediately. Eating her pleasant fruits and delighting in her love and obedience refreshed Him. She is His sister, His bride. Her focus is on satisfying Him, not on serving herself.

Earlier in 1:6, she had neglected her own inner life, but now she is a banquet table for others. She had been feasting on Him, abiding in Him, and now others can feast on the luscious fruit the Spirit produced within her.

Her friends delight in seeing the maiden's passionate love for her Bridegroom.

Selah: Jesus delights in your love for Him, your desire to please Him, your gratefulness for His sacrificial death, your enjoyment of His presence. Do as the maiden did in 4:16 and invite Him to enjoy you.

Come Sweet Jesus, Come!

The Cost to Follow Jesus

The maiden discovers it costs to follow Jesus who gave His all for her. He asks if she is willing to give her all for Him. Will she follow Him even if the journey is difficult?

Beloved

5:2 I slept but my heart was awake. Listen! My lover is knocking: "Open to me, my sister, my darling, my dove, my flawless one. My head is drenched with dew, my hair with the dampness of the night."

Jesus knocks on the door of her heart in answer to her prayer in Song 4:16 for the north winds. But after her mountaintop experience, she did what many of us do. Perhaps she became contented with her past experiences of grace. She seemed to be somewhat self-indulgent and self-occupied.

When Jesus spoke to the Laodicean church, he was speaking to His people who had grown lukewarm, and He stood outside the door hoping for admittance. "Here I am! I stand at the door and knock. If anyone hears my voice and opens the door, I will come in and eat with him, and he with me" (Revelation 3:20). It is sad that He is outside a closed door and should need to knock. But love of ease always closes the door. Yet her heart is not far from Him, and when He spoke, she was close enough to hear Him.

He begins in a most loving way describing her with four endearments. She was His sister and He could identify with her. "I, too, was tempted, so I understand."

She was His darling. "How I love you! Let My love for you be your motivation."

She was His dove. "I am so pleased that in you I see sincerity, purity, gentleness, and the single-minded beauty of the dove."

She was His flawless one. "I see Your desire to please me and that makes you perfect in My eyes."

His head drenched with dew and His hair with the dampness of the night remind us of the hours He spent in the Garden of Gethsemane. He is coming to her as a Man of Sorrows calling her to experience sacrifice and rejection. (Isaiah 53:4b) Will she welcome and go with this aspect of her Lover? Will she be willing to share in His sufferings? (Philippians 3:10)

Earlier she had enjoyed Him as the sweet Savior with whom she enjoyed communion under the apple tree. Then He had said, "Come with me" (2:13). To do that she had to get rid of the little foxes that were causing the shadows in her life. She obeyed after a painful separation.

Now He is asking for a closer intimacy than she had ever known. He comes with a different call: "Open to me." He is asking to be permitted to come into her.

This is what He asks of us. Will we allow Him to fully indwell us, to abide in us? No longer will we decide what to do, where to go, where to live. He's asking us to give Him the right to make those and all other choices for us.

Several weeks after Elsie Blake (later Kinlaw) met Jesus as a student at Asbury College, Elsie heard Jesus whisper, "You have given me your heart; would you give me your whole life?" She answered quickly: "Oh, Jesus, Yes!"

After that, Elsie's life was marked by a passionate love for Jesus, for people, and for service. Those commitments that Elsie made to Jesus determined every other decision she made, and became the cornerstone for all that Jesus would do with her life. (Read more of Elsie's commitment to Jesus in Appendix D.)

Selah: This is the question confronting every one who has given her heart to Jesus. Write your commitment to give Him your whole life. What will that include for you?

Jesus, I give you my life, my health, my wealth, my home, my family, my relationships, my heart, my body, my soul, my thoughts. Please help me to want Your approval over man's approval always.

5:3 I have taken off my robe—must I put it on again? I have washed my feet—must I soil them again?

It seems that she is counting the cost. She felt she had good reasons not to go.

The little word "I" appears four times in this verse. She is saying to the One to whom she had pledged her love, "You know I love You, but I need to sleep right now." She speaks of "my robe" and "my feet" showing she has not totally yielded control of them. Perhaps her surrender was not as complete as she had thought.

Jesus was in all points tempted as we are, and in the garden of Gethsemane he said, "If it be possible, let this cup pass away from Me: nevertheless, not as I will, but as Thou wilt" (Matthew 26:39).

It is here that many Christians fail to go on and experience the deep life Christ has for them. Through fear of consequences, fear of the unknown, fear of being deprived of familiar comforts, and fear of suffering, they hesitate and some never open the door when the nail scarred hand knocks. Today in many places, they know that if they follow Jesus, they may lose their jobs or even their lives.

Jesus will never force anyone to open to Him and to follow when persecuted. He will only knock and ask. But neither is He ever vague about His requirements. He knows exactly what we must surrender in order for us to be completely open to His reign in our hearts. He wants to know, "Do you love me more than this?"

Vickie and her boyfriend knelt in our family room, asked Jesus into their hearts, and found the joy of having their sins forgiven. A few months later Vickie learned of the need to allow the Spirit to have full control of her life. As she prayed, the Holy Spirit asked if she would be willing not to wear the beautiful wedding dress she had purchased. Vickie said that as a girl she had not had a lot of pretty clothes, and her wedding dress was dear to her heart.

It was a struggle, but finally she surrendered the wedding dress. If God said not to wear it, she would not. With that surrender, she opened her heart to Him with no reservations. His Spirit filled her spirit. She realized later that God had not forbid her to wear the dress but had asked if she was willing not to wear it. Vickie walked down the aisle in a very sacred ceremony in her beautiful wedding dress.

God knows what our "wedding dress" is. For Abraham, it was Isaac, his much-loved son of promise. God was asking Abraham to surrender all his ideas about how God was going to fulfill His promise to bless him.

When Abraham surrendered Isaac, God didn't need to ask, "Now, Abraham, what about that land or those sheep?" God knew Isaac represented Abraham's total surrender. That is always what He seeks. He knows if we surrender what is most dear, He is welcome to come in as Lord of all.

Selah: "Now I know that you fear God, because you have not withheld from me your son, your only son" (Genesis 22:12). Rewrite this verse inserting what you believe the Holy Spirit would say represents your Isaac or your wedding dress. Do you love Jesus more than your "wedding dress" or your "Isaac?"

Now I know that You love me more because you have let go of trying to resolve your relationship w/ your Dad.

5:4 My lover thrust his hand through the latch-opening; my heart began to pound for him.

The doors had holes in them allowing a person to reach through and unlock the door. He puts His nail-pierced hand through the door letting her know He is doing all He can to reveal Himself to her. She had been so overwhelmed with His love for her, is she ready to go wherever He leads her? She promised to do whatever He asked. Is she truly willing? She's learning that there is a price for intimacy with God. Is she willing to pay it?

The words "my heart began to pound for him" means "my inner being was moved for Him." The phrase is used to express sympathy and affection, especially with tender regret. She was sad she had wounded His heart. She had counted the cost. Yes, she truly loves Him more than all else and all others.

Selah: Are you willing to pay the price for intimacy with God? What do you think it might cost you?

Yes! Pride + Fear — of which I want none!

What will be the benefits?

Freedom in Christ, in truth, in Love!

5:5 I arose to open for my lover, and my hands dripped with myrrh, my fingers with flowing myrrh, on the handles of the lock.

She does arise! She will open to Him! The myrrh on the doorknob that then drips from her hand reminds her of the suffering of her Bridegroom. It is now on her hands, and her response is a wholehearted "Yes!" She is willing to suffer with Him. Myrrh, the ointment that was a fragrant burial spice with a bitter taste, speaks of death to self and of the commitment to embrace the cross.

She has decided to follow Him no matter the cost. When she looked at the nail scarred hand, she could not ignore Him. She arises in obedience.

Living for Christ is like the wine mingled with myrrh. If we take the cup the Lord gives us to drink, even though it may appear to represent hardship, pain or loneliness, we shall find that the aroma of it in the end is incredibly sweet.

5:6 I opened for my lover, but my lover had left; he was gone. My heart sank at his departure. I looked for him but did not find him. I called him but he did not answer.

Her heart sank because He had departed. This is not an attack of the devil but the sovereign purpose of God being worked out in her life to cause her to mature.

He had invited her to go out into the night with Him— the night is where the lost and broken people are. She hesitated as she counted the cost, but her answer is, "Yes!" She loves Him and will follow. He saw that her hesitation to open was not because she was unwilling. In the center of her will she is steadfastly purposed to follow Him at any cost.

We may have times when it seems God has forsaken us, but God never does forsake us. It is only that He seems to be away. "Truly you are a God who hides himself" (Isaiah 45:15).

The primary thing Satan wants to destroy when we go through a testing time is our faith. When it seems God is not aware of our struggles, will we continue to trust that He is in control, that He loves us, and that He allows only what is best?

Selah: When have you gone through a dark place in *several* which it seems that God did not answer your prayers? Did *times* your faith remain strong during the test? *—yes!*

In what way do such struggles benefit us?

Deepen our trust in relying on God, not ourselves

5:7 The watchmen found me as they made their rounds in the city. They beat me, they bruised me; they took away my cloak, those watchmen of the walls!

The leaders of the church, who should have protected her, persecuted her. They took away her cloak exposing her sorrows to others. Her sensitive spirit knew that they whispered about her and wholly misjudged the cause of her suffering. They should have shielded her from Satan's attacks by assuring her of God's promises to keep her and to reassure her that His presence would return.

Instead, they assumed she had done something wrong and so they hit her with their accusations. Rather than shield her from others, they exposed her failure for all to see as they said to others in the church, "You need to pray for her. Did you know...?"

Like Job's friends they gathered round her, intending to help or comfort, but they wounded her all the more. The psalmist said, "I looked for sympathy, but there was none, for comforters, but I found none" (Psalm 69:20).

True keepers of the wall say, "You are loved! Your Lord is coming! He is delighted with your earnest desire to find

Him. He has something good in this for you. Don't give up."

But Satan accuses. "You failed Him now. He doesn't want to help you. You don't deserve His presence. You might as well give up."

Sometimes our Sovereign Lord sees that to delay is giving us His best answer. We should not believe that delay means denial, and we should refuse to allow Satan to shake our confidence in God. Unanswered prayers are not unheard. God keeps a record of every prayer we pray.

The Lord had captivated her heart, and she was earnestly searching for Him, rather than frantically seeking His blessings, as in the past. She recognized that the Lord was allowing her to be chastened for her good. "For whom the Lord loves He chastens" (Hebrews 12:6).

The Lord left her in this difficulty until He brought about the necessary changes in her. She was now able to believe that the Lord works "all things together for good" and was able to maintain a good attitude despite the watchmen. "But he knows the way that I take; when he has tested me, I will come forth as gold" (Job 23:10).

There is value in suffering. One lady wrote: "Many times I have tried to run from the suffering. But God seems to keep bringing the suffering my way until I learn to suffer for Him. I am learning to grab hold of the suffering, realizing that it cleanses me of myself. I want to be like Him! Suffering is the only way.

"I heard that when we get to heaven, God won't look for the applause we had on this earth, or the diplomas, or wealth. He will only be looking for the scars. I want to bear the scars of suffering for Him.

"I am learning that I can have joy, even in the midst of the suffering. He is teaching me to rest under His wing; there I find peace."

She signed it "Rejoicing in my portion…"

"Be truly glad. There is wonderful joy ahead, even though you have to endure many trials for a little while. These trials will show that your faith is genuine. It is being tested as fire tests and purifies gold—though your faith is far more precious than mere gold. So when your faith remains strong through many trials, it will bring you much praise and glory and honor on the day when Jesus Christ is revealed to the whole world" (1 Peter 1:6-7 NLT).

Selah: Can you think of a time when you had only God to depend on? Perhaps others didn't know or understand your situation. What is most helpful—or damaging—to faith in such times?

Yes!

Staying my gaze on Him + Reading Scripture, praying.

5:8 O daughters of Jerusalem, I charge you—if you find my lover, what will you tell him? Tell him I am faint with love.

His presence is nowhere to be found. She is as Job was when he said, "So I looked for good, but evil came instead. I waited for the light, but darkness fell" (Job 30:26 NLT). Still despite all of the hurt and rejection, she does not blame Him. Instead, she calls to the daughters of Jerusalem to tell Him that she is faint with love. She wants Him more than she wants anything else. Perhaps they would find Him and give Him a message for her.

She had earlier said she was sick of love because the joy of His love was almost too great for her. But that time His banner over her was love. Now He is absent, and it is her longing for the absent Bridegroom that produces her heart-sickness. Her love for Him is so intense that she cannot bear the prospect of losing Him. If He only knew her yearning for Him, He would return.

It is remarkable that she does not say one word of bitterness or complaint toward those who heaped criticisms upon her. When we have been wounded by a spouse, a son or daughter, a parent, a friend, a church minister or fellow worker, it can be almost unbearable. As Proverbs 18:14 states, "A crushed spirit who can bear?" Yet it is possible to forgive because Jesus has carried all of our sorrows and griefs (Isaiah 53:4-5). "The insults of those who insult you have fallen on me" (Romans 15:3).

Selah: If there is someone you can't forgive, ask Jesus for grace to say, "I allow You to forgive through me as You forgave Your persecutors while hanging on the cross. I will be a channel of Your forgiveness."

The Beauty of Jesus

The maiden has passed the ultimate test. She trusts and loves Him even after she has been unable to find Him and has been mistreated by others.

When her friends imply that He is no better than any other (5:9), her soul is stirred to its depths. She begins to pour forth a portrayal of Him that is comparable to the descriptions of the Ancient of Days in Daniel 7:9-10 and of our risen Lord in Revelation 1:13-16. Her words guide our praises. As we praise Him, we, too, enter into His presence.

Friends

5:9 How is your beloved better than others, most beautiful of women? How is your beloved better than others, that you charge us so?

The maiden's remarkable response to testing is not lost on her friends. They cannot understand such devotion. She

83

has been mistreated by others and seemingly ignored by her Lover. Yet she refuses to be offended. In fact, she pleads, "I charge you, O daughters of Jerusalem, If you find my beloved, That you tell him I *am* lovesick!" (NKJV).

In amazement they ask, "How can you be so in love with One who treats you like this? Tell us the secret?"

They call her "most beautiful of women." They have a deep respect for her because she has remained loyal during the most difficult time in her life. During our most severe testing is often the time others see Jesus in us most clearly. They recognize that our response is not what theirs would be in similar circumstances.

If we had been mistreated as she was and we were asked to describe Jesus, what would be our response? Would we give a wholehearted praise of His faithfulness? If we speak of Him with unwavering love, we will find, as she did, that we have the joy of being restored to His presence.

The best way to maintain faith during our trials is to focus on Jesus and to praise Him for His unfailing love and to think deeply on His supreme superlatives. And this is what she does. While she is telling others, she is engrossed in the wonder of Him. Nothing brings us through the dark times better than to have our eyes on the attributes of God and His matchless qualities.

Selah: Think of a difficult period in your life. If you had been asked to describe what Jesus meant to you during that time, what would have been your response?

Do you know someone whose faith during testing has been an inspiration to you?

5:10 My lover is radiant and ruddy, outstanding among ten thousand.

Instead of doubting His love because she does not enjoy a sense of His presence, the maiden begins to think on what she knows to be true of Him. At God's chosen time, He will make her aware that He is very near.

She names ten things mentioning first a general statement. The qualities she mentions guide our praises.

How is it possible to describe the One who is the radiance of God's glory and the exact representation of His being (Hebrews 1:3)? The word "radiant" means dazzling white. White is a combination of all colors. Jesus is the culmination of all perfections.

He isn't just one of many. He is the best, the indescribable among tens of thousands. In the Hebrew ten thousand is used as a superlative. In everything He has the supremacy. (Colossians 1:18 NLT)

The word "ruddy" was used of a garment stained with blood. Jesus' sacred body was reddened with His precious blood. We praise Him for the perfect beauty of His holy life that was a picture of holiness such as the world had never seen and such as no human intellect could have imagined. But it was His death that He said would draw all men to Himself (John 12:32).

What follows are the holy descriptions of why she finds Him to be everything to her.

5:11 His head is purest gold; his hair is wavy and black as a raven.

His head of pure gold refers to the Divine leadership He has over everything. "He guides me in paths of righteousness for his name's sake" (Psalm 23:3). She joyfully exclaims, "He loves me and He has absolute authority over me! He guides every detail of my life!"

Black hair portrays His eternal and unfading power. When the Bible describes a man's condition as degenerating, it speaks of his gray hair (Hosea 7:9). But our Lord is the same yesterday, today and forever (Hebrews 13:8). "I am the LORD, and I do not change" (Malachi 3:6). His love, wisdom and power will never fade. When He gives us a promise, He has already seen the future and knows He can keep it. He cannot be talked into answering selfish prayers. God never changes moods or cools off in His affections. He never loses His enthusiasm for us.

Selah: Praise Him for His ability to lead and rule every detail of your life. What are specific times you know He led you? Divorcing Mike

5:12 His eyes are like doves by the water streams, washed in milk mounted like jewels.

She remembers that He looks at her with great love. His eyes are pure and clear with a moistness in them that expresses loving tenderness. Her heart melts as she remembers that even when He discerns her hidden sins, His eyes fill with compassion.

Scripture says that even though the rich young ruler would not follow Him, "Jesus looked at him and loved him" (Mark 10:21). We often underestimate the love Jesus has for us when we fail.

His eyes are washed in milk. Milk is nourishing and refreshing and the look of love in His eyes nourished and refreshed her. In His eyes, she saw gentleness, purity, and the love of the Holy Spirit. Just as a dove fixes its eye only on its mate, so the maiden sees that the eyes of the Lord are fixed on her. He made her feel that she was the most special one in the world.

His eyes have ability to see everything about us—even our hidden motives, thoughts and desires. He sees our past and our future, but His eyes always look upon us with love.

Others may change their attitude toward us, but His attitude toward us never wavers. We can go to Him at any time without wondering whether we'll find Him in a receptive mood.

Selah: What expression do you think Jesus has when He looks at you? *Mercy + Compassion + forgiveness*

Is Jesus pleased with your concept of His attitude toward you? *yes*

5:13 His cheeks are like beds of spice yielding perfume.

Many interpretations have been given to the word "cheeks," but I especially like the reference to it in *Pulpit* Commentary as meaning "countenance." The priests were to bless the Israelites with these words:

"The Lord bless you and keep you;

"The Lord make His face shine upon you, And be gracious to you;

"The Lord lift up His countenance upon you, And give you peace." (Numbers 6:24-26 NKJV).

The word "countenance" refers to God's face repeatedly in Scripture. "Let the light of your face shine upon us, O LORD" (Psalm 4:6). When the light of God's face shines upon us, we have His favor.

Selah: When God told the priests to bless the Israelites with the blessing in Numbers 6:24-26 (above), He promised, "Whenever Aaron and his sons bless the people of Israel in my name, I myself will bless them" (Numbers 6:27). Pray this blessing for those in your family, and praise Him for the peace His favor gives.

His lips are like lilies dripping with myrrh.

Lilies have a sweet fragrance. "Everyone spoke well of him and was amazed by the gracious words that came from his lips" (Luke 4:22).

His lips drop myrrh; every gracious word He speaks is based on His death. Whether he says, "Your sins are forgiven," (Luke 7:48) or "Your faith has healed you. Go in peace" (Luke 8:48), His death made those statements possible.

His words always encourage us to embrace the Cross and die to self. Yet, even when He speaks convicting words, we sense loving concern.

One night when I was a teenager, strong accusations filled my mind telling me I was not really the Christian I professed to be. The words came so forcefully to my mind, that I was confused and frightened.

The next morning in tears I told an older lady about the accusations. She calmed my fears by teaching me how to discern between Satan's voice and God's. "Satan's voice comes with force, often demanding an immediate response. God's voice is gentle."

God's voice gives us clear direction, but Satan's causes confusion. "God is not the author of confusion, but of peace" (1 Corinthians 14:33 NKJV).

If we are seeking to discern God's will and lack clear direction, we should wait. God gives us time. God says, "This is what you ought to do." Satan demands, "This is what you have to do!" If there is intense pressure associated with the thought, reject it as either your own mind or a satanic tactic.

When thoughts bring a helpless, hopeless, all-is-lost feeling, that is not God's voice.

Selah: Have you sensed Jesus speaking to you regarding a needed change? If so, were the words harsh or tender?

At times are you confused about who is putting thoughts into your mind? If so, which of the points above can be helpful?

What are other ways to discern if thoughts that come to us are from God, Satan, or our own mind?

5:14 His hands are rods of gold set with beryl.

How comforting to remember that no one can snatch her out of His hands (John 10:28). She alone had the power to leave His loving hold. His holy hands are rods of gold. Everything His hands accomplish is pure, powerful and glorious.

Beryl is mentioned several times in Scripture including Ezekiel 1:16 and Daniel 10:6. In these places, the meaning is stability.

His hands have you, your loved ones, and all that concerns you firmly in His care.

His body is like polished ivory decorated with sapphires (NKJV).

The Hebrew word for "body" means inward parts and is sometimes used figuratively to represent emotion or compassion. So His "body" speaks of deep feelings or tender concern. There is no one like Jesus who is filled with kindness for each of us.

"I have compassion on the multitude, because they have now continued with Me three days and have nothing to eat" (Mark 8:2 NKJV). The Bible speaks five times of Jesus' compassion for the multitudes. He had pity on the individuals also, such as the bereaved (Luke 7:12-13) and the sick (Mark 1:40-41).

Selah: Worship Him as you recall times His compassion made a difference in your life. Who has He used to express His loving concern to you?

5:15 His legs are pillars of marble set on bases of pure gold.

Jesus' legs speak of His steadfast strength. Their pure gold bases are the foundation of His Divine power. He does not fail to accomplish all He desires. Nothing can stop Him when He is determined to act!

His appearance is like Lebanon, choice as its cedars.

His appearance is as full of majesty and beauty as the cedars of Lebanon. Looking at Him was truly awe-inspiring—both to herself and to her friends who were listening to her.

We, too, are changed as we look on Him. As we remember His unsurpassed beauty, the enemy's lies become faint. We begin to sense, as she did, that He is not far from us.

Selah: Since He loves to hear our words of love to Him, take one minute to write down all the words you can think of to describe Him. Then read or sing them as a prayer of worship. *Tender, beautiful, magnificent, Alpha, Omega, Healer, physician, Shepherd, friend, Savior, King, Companion, Loyal, Loving, Kindhearted, Passionate, devoted, Zealous*

5:16 His mouth is sweetness itself; he is altogether lovely. This is my lover, this my friend, O daughters of Jerusalem.

"How sweet your words taste to me; they are sweeter than honey" (Psalm 119:103). Every other pleasure fades in comparison to one kiss of sacred intimacy. It is the most pleasing experience known to the human spirit. His Words transform us. Even the temple guards said, "No one ever spoke the way this man does" (John 7:46). His words are full of truth and loving-kindness.

By the end of her speaking, her words are full of feelings. It is as if she is joyfully singing, "He is altogether lovely. This is my lover; this is my friend." She has learned the power of speaking His praise. Her mountain of despair had disappeared!

The daughters of Jerusalem must have been amazed. She came to them in shame, but now they can see that just speaking about her Lover has lifted her head, and she rejoices as she thinks of how wonderful He is.

Isobel Kuhn tells in her book *Green Leaf in Drought* of the Matthews who were missionaries in China when Communism overtook the country. Other missionaries were allowed to leave, but they and their small daughter were left alone with barely enough money to survive. Their clothes grew ragged, and their food supply became so poor that even the Chinese felt pity. For months they prayed earnestly for release and claimed God's promises for deliverance. But this "claiming" only wore them out and made them restless.

Then one day it occurred to Arthur that Jesus had left heaven, not just to fulfill the will of God, but also to delight in doing what His Father wanted. Up to now they had not really submitted. Instead, they thought they should be claiming His promises. Their prayers had selfishly centered around shortening their days in China.

They knelt before the Lord and joyfully abandoned themselves to do His will. They would gladly stay in that little room as long as He wished them to.

The peace of God poured in like a flood. Arthur wrote to people who had been praying for their release and quoted the words, "Thou hast kept the best wine till now." Delighting in Jesus gave them more joy than a mere deliverance would have provided. Arthur and Wilda began to praise God and to gladly cry with the psalmist, "I delight to do thy will, O my God" (Psalm 40:8 KJV).

Selah: Why is the best gift during testing often not relief from the situation, but grace to endure joyfully as the Matthews did? Have you experienced such a time?

Has there been a time when you praised God while you were going through a deep trial? What were the results?

Jesus Delights in His Garden

The daughters of Jerusalem had just asked, "Who is He?"
After hearing her glorious description of Him, they ask, "Where
is He?" They are ready to join in pursuit of this One who is so
wonderful.

Friends

6:1 Where has your lover gone, O woman of rare beauty?
Which way did he turn so we can help you find him? (NLT)
    The enemy knows the power that can flow through the
life of one who praises God despite hardship. We are still
blessed by Job who endured great loss and could say,
"When he tests me, I will come out as pure as gold" (Job
23:10 NLT).
    Others are watching to see if we go through great
difficulties and can still testify, "Despite all these things,
overwhelming victory is ours through Christ, who loved

us" (Romans 8:37 NLT). Those who live victoriously come what may, exercise an attractive force towards God.

Selah: Paul wrote: "For your sake we face death all day long; we are considered as sheep to be slaughtered. No, in all these things we are more than conquerors through him who loved us" (Romans 8:37-38).

What words in those verses explain why Paul was "more than conqueror" during difficult days?

He remains in Christ's love

Beloved

6:2 My beloved has gone down to his garden, to the beds of spices, to browse in the gardens and to gather lilies.

As she ponders their question, suddenly she knows! "He is in His garden. I am His garden. He is within me!" Although it seemed that He left, He only retreated from her feelings. In reality He is still within her.

Notice that this verse first uses the word "garden," then "gardens." Jesus loves His garden. All of us who are His are one body (garden) with many individual smaller, lovely gardens making up this one glorious garden. "The body is not made up of one part but of many" (1 Corinthians 12:14).

The garden of the Lord is His Church. Jesus loves to be with His people. He does not wait until we are without mistakes; He comes when we desire Him.

"The beds of spices" speak of the different ones in His church. We are all like various spices. He takes great pleasure in the diversity of His garden. The Lord wants us to value those who have differing personalities, gifts, and graces.

Selah: Do you have trouble appreciating those who are unlike you? Think of them as being a different spice or a different flower in God's garden. He enjoys the variety and will help you do the same.

6:3 I am my beloved's and my beloved is mine; he browses among the lilies.

This statement is similar to her earlier "My beloved is mine and I am his"—yet there's an important difference. Then her first thought was of her claim upon Christ; His claim upon her was secondary. Now she thinks first of His claim and only afterward mentions her own claim. The focus of her life has now turned to Jesus.

Our own enjoyment of Him is our marvelous privilege. But as we mature in love, we will realize that the thirst of His heart is to commune with His Bride.

No sooner has she acknowledged herself as His possession than He appears. He tells her how beautiful she is in His eyes.

The gathering of lilies may refer to His receiving the prayers and praises of His people. Jesus has deep pleasure as His people express their love to Him. He goes to the garden to refresh himself by communing with those who love Him. Fellowshipping with His loved ones was the joy that was set before Him when He endured the pain of the cross. "Because of the joy awaiting him, he endured the cross, disregarding its shame" (Hebrews 12:2-3 NLT).

Selah: What difference would it make if you consistently remembered that Jesus suffered on the cross so He could have the joy of your loving fellowship?

To Not put it last but to put our fellowshipping first always,

6:4 You are as beautiful as Tirzah, my darling, as lovely as Jerusalem, as majestic as troops with banners.

When an army in the ancient world returned victorious from battle, they displayed their banners in a military parade. A defeated army lost its banners. She had defeated her greatest enemies, because during her testing time she did not give in to sin and unbelief.

6:5 Turn your eyes from me; they overwhelm me.

The look of love in her eyes moved Him deeply. When the daughters asked, "Why do you love Him?" she spoke of Him as being altogether lovely after she had gone through the most difficult test of her life. Her steadfast look of devotion during her difficult season overcame Him.

When we unwaveringly love Him in the midst of our pain, His heart is moved beyond description. He tells her to stop gazing at Him, as if to say, "I can't take it anymore." Her love overwhelmed His heart. Our greatest glory is that we can move God's heart. Jesus made the universe—the stars, the planets, the galaxies—but none of creation's beauty overwhelms Him as we do!

When we pursue Him in the midst of our pain, when we do not think doubtful thoughts if He fails to show up when we want Him to, He says, "Turn your eyes away, for they overpower me." (NLT)

She has yet to come out of the wilderness leaning on her Lover, yet she has the capacity to ravish the heart of God! One of the great revelations of the Song is that even weak and incomplete believers can overwhelm God's heart.

Selah: Do you feel especially weak or tested? Then take time to praise Him and tell Him how much you adore Him. Your love for Him in the midst of testing is more precious to Him than you can comprehend.

Your hair is like a flock of goats descending from Gilead.

6:6 Your teeth are like a flock of sheep coming up from the washing. Each has its twin, not one of them is missing.

6:7 Your temples behind your veil are like the halves of a pomegranate.

There are more verses describing King Solomon's admiration of the lowly maiden than verses expressing her esteem for him. No matter how much we esteem Jesus, His delight in us exceeds all we can imagine.

As she listens to Him, she matures spiritually. The qualities He mentions are those that develop in us when we immerse ourselves in His Word.

Jesus described her spiritual maturity by highlighting three things: her dedication (hair), life in the Word (teeth) and pure motives (temples). These are the same qualities that he mentioned earlier when these qualities were only beginning to form.

Her fruitful ministry and her balanced approach to Truth come from her feeding on Scripture. Again, He mentions that her motives are pure and beautiful in His sight.

Selah: Every feature speaks of her spiritual growth. Her dedication, love for His Word, pure motives and belief in His goodness during testing are indications of her maturity. Compare these qualities with those others might use to judge us.

6:8 Sixty queens there may be, and eighty concubines, and virgins beyond number;

6:9 but my dove, my perfect one, is unique, the only daughter of her mother, the favorite of the one who bore her. The young women saw her and called her blessed; the queens and concubines praised her.

6:10 Who is this that appears like the dawn, fair as the moon, bright as the sun, majestic as the stars in procession?

Jesus proclaims that no one compares to the bride in the heavenly court. His bride has more honor than all the hosts in Heaven. In God's court are groups such as the seraphim, cherubim, and archangels, but He gives her more glory than all others.

He is saying, "She is more special to Me than all of the attendants in My court. She is the one I would die for." The love of Jesus is so powerful that He can look at each one who pursues Him and call that one unique.

The question "Who is this...?" appears three times in this book (3:6, 6:10, 8:5). The word "this" is feminine so the question is, "Who is she?"

She appears "like the dawn." The dawn signals a new beginning, a new start in the things of God.

She is "fair as the moon" or as beautiful as the full moon. The moon continually reflects the light of the sun. Its glory is totally the glory of another! Just as the moon uses no energy to bless, so we are not to struggle in our energy to live the Christian life, but each day we totally rely upon the Lord to touch others through us.

She is "bright as the sun." The Hebrew word means "clear." The clear light of God shines through her. He has chosen us to reflect His glory—to be those through whom others see His purity and love.

She is as "majestic as the stars in procession." The stars are compared to warriors in Judges 5:20: "The stars in their orbits fought against Sisera" (NLT). His lovely bride is like an army overcoming the powers of darkness.

Selah: Jesus notices every detail about each of us. He continually enjoys and admires our efforts to please Him. Write what comes to your mind when you ask Him what He most loves about you.

?

Compelled by Love

The bride responds to His loving admiration with enthusiasm to serve and with beautiful humility.

Beloved

6:11 I went down to the grove of nut trees to look at the new growth in the valley, to see if the vines had budded or the pomegranates were in bloom.

She goes down not only to look but also to intercede for others. Her self-consumed attitude is being replaced with a mature love for the church. She is quick to recognize their strengths and potential for fruitfulness. She is one with her Lord as she engages in His service.

Selah: A mark of spiritual maturity is turning our attention to the spiritual growth of others. What will be evidences that we have concern for the spiritual life of those around us? Serving & praying for others

6:12 Before I realized it, my desire set me among the royal chariots of my people.

She suddenly found she had great zeal for others and enthusiasm to serve God's people. Instead of being put off by the immaturity, pride, wrong applications of the Word and lack of discernment of those less mature, she is now surprised by the tender compassion she feels. She becomes compelled by love. (2 Corinthians 5:11, 14)

Selah: Do you tend to look at other believers' strengths or their weaknesses? What helps you to focus on their strengths? Asking to see others through Jesus' eyes

Friends

6:13 Return, return, O Shulammite; Return, return, that we may look upon you! (NKJV)

For the first time she is called "Shulammite"—the feminine form of Solomon, the Prince of Peace. How appropriate that they call her by His name for she now bears His image more than ever before. Her concerns reflect His.

Those who have the life of Jesus in them are the ones who are missed when they depart. The friends cry out, "Come back, come back, come back! Let me gaze upon Jesus in you once again for it is so refreshing to my soul." They repeat their call showing their intense desire. They see her love for others and wish to be near her so they can learn from her.

Mature saints are the truly attractive ones to others in the Body of Christ. It is sometimes easier for those with immature faith to see Jesus if they see Him through the mature ones.

Selah: Can you think of a mature believer people gravitate towards? What traits characterize that person's life? Compassion, humility, vulnerability

Will you pray, "Dear Bridegroom of my heart, cause me to be so intimate with You that Your presence in me will have a positive spiritual effect on others"? yes!

Beloved

What would you see in the Shulammite—As it were, the dance of the two camps? (NKJV)

Her beauty amazes her friends. Christ' love for her has caused her to love Him, and now her happy love for Him gives her a rare loveliness that they admire.

But the Shulammite cannot conceive why any attention should be paid to her. "What will you see in her?" The eager look of the daughters of Jerusalem surprised the bride.

The word "camps" can be translated as "Mahanaim" which was the place of Jacob's encounter with angels in Genesis 32:2. The word must have come to mean a very exciting place that attracted people. Dancing in Scripture is a sign of victory. "When the victorious Israelite army was returning home after David had killed the Philistine, women from all the towns of Israel came out to meet King Saul. They sang and danced for joy with tambourines and cymbals" (1 Samuel 18:6; also Exodus 15:20).

So, the dance of two camps or armies refers to a victory dance. In her perfect modesty and humility, she is unaware of how beautiful she really is. "Why do you look at the Shulammite as though you were gazing at two heavenly armies celebrating a victory dance?"

Selah: Humility is an important quality in the spiritually mature. What are evidences someone is humble? How do you think humility is obtained?

They don't call attention to themselves

dying to selfishness

Lover

7:1 How beautiful your sandaled feet, O prince's daughter! Your graceful legs are like jewels, the work of a craftsman's hands.

7:2 Your navel is a rounded goblet that never lacks blended wine. Your waist is a mound of wheat encircled by lilies.

Her Lover explains the marvelous virtues in her that are so amazingly attractive, not just to Him but also to those who long for her to be near them. He repeats qualities mentioned earlier but adds her ability to walk in truth and wisdom, her dependence upon Him, her keen discernment, her thought life, and her increased fruitfulness.

In 4:1-5 her Bridegroom gave eight affirmations beginning with her head. He now gives ten. These ten virtues are a practical definition of godliness. They are in us also when we meditate and apply the Word.

For the first time the Beloved describes His bride's feet. She is now striving to walk "in step with the Spirit" (Galatians 5:25). She is ready and willing to go with Him anywhere. When we carefully follow Him, we give Him great pleasure: "I have no greater joy than to hear that my children are walking in the truth" (3 John 1:4).

Her shoes speak of evangelism. "How beautiful on the mountains are the feet of those who bring good news" (Isaiah 52:7). Her graceful legs like jewels speak of her ability to walk in Christ's power and wisdom.

The word "naval" is the Hebrew word for "umbilical cord," so the naval is the lifeline to her spiritual life. She has learned to be totally dependent upon Him. Her inner life is the result of her attachment to Him. Because she is continually dependent, she is full of the wine of the Holy Spirit. The mound of wheat is a picture of the abundance of the harvest.

Selah: He has praised her for keeping in step with the Spirit, for walking in Christ's power, and learning to continually depend upon the Spirit.

In which of these areas do you most desire to improve? What will help you? *All three*

⤷ Being silent in prayer + listening for His word

7:3 Your breasts are like two fawns, twins of a gazelle.

He repeats the words He spoke in 4:5. 1 Thessalonians 5:8 unlocks the secret of the two breasts. "But since we belong to the day, let us be self-controlled, putting on faith and love as a breastplate." She is filled equally with faith and love. She needs both as she ministers to others.

The words "which feed among the lilies" that were in 4:5 are omitted here. Feeding among the lilies refers to enjoying the fellowship of other surrendered lilies. The Holy Spirit feeds our spirits through others as we share about Jesus. However, the spiritually mature believer does not need to depend on that fellowship for spiritual sustenance. Jesus alone can satisfy her spiritually.

Spirit-filled surrender results in allowing Jesus to fill all our needs when fellowship with others is not available. Madame Jeanne Guyon, a 17th century Christian imprisoned for her faith, dearly loved Song of Songs, and one of her books is written describing its beauties. Her deep love relationship with Jesus caused her to survive the many long years of imprisonment where she lived in a cell below ground level. She had no light except a candle at mealtime. After ten years in this place she wrote:

A little bird I am, shut from the fields of air;
Yet in my cage I sit and sing to Him who placed
    me there;
Well pleased a prisoner to be,
Because, my God, it pleases Thee!

Selah: Do you depend more upon your friends for spiritual support or upon the Lord? *The Lord for sure!*

What do you think it means to be able to say, "The LORD is my portion" (Lamentations 3:24)? or "All my fountains are in you" (Psalm 87:7). *Jesus is enough!! ♡*

7:4 Your neck is like an ivory tower. Your eyes are the pools of Heshbon by the gate of Bath Rabbim. Your nose is like the tower of Lebanon looking toward Damascus.

As mentioned earlier, the neck in Scripture represents the human will. This speaks of her resolute determination that has become her protection from evil. She is meek and yielding in all matters concerning herself but unbending in faithfulness to her Lord.

In 4:4 He described her neck as the tower of David, now it is like an ivory tower. An ivory tower is a symbol for noble purity and speaks of her pure desires. His will is her will. She is determined to carry out His desires and to bring glory to Him rather than to herself.

It is amazing that we can speak with our eyes without saying a word. We can look into someone's eyes and detect joy, love, hate, understanding, depression, confusion. Pools are still, quiet waters. Her eyes have a spiritual depth to them.

The nose speaks of discernment, intuitive knowledge of God that can be likened to the sense of smell. The nose warns if there is a gas leak or an electrical wire burning. It alerts us to dangers that cannot be seen or heard.

Discernment is the virtue that is the quickest to be dulled by any act of disobedience.

The tower of Lebanon was a watchtower built to detect the enemy's activities. The maiden is now mature enough to discern the enemy's tactics. Her supernatural discernment in spiritual warfare will be a source of protection from the enemy. Without keen discernment, we are vulnerable to the strategies of darkness.

Her nose is pointed toward Damascus, the city that was the seat of Israel's perpetual enemy, Syria. This tower looked out over the valley or plain in order to spot enemy movements from afar. A discerning believer is one who becomes aware of the enemy. The Holy Spirit gives sensitivity to recognize the enemy's tactics.

When Solomon prayed for discernment, God was greatly pleased. "So God said to him, 'Since you have asked for this and not for long life or wealth for yourself...I will do what you have asked. I will give you a wise and discerning heart, so that there will never have been anyone like you, nor will there ever be. Moreover, I will give you what you have not asked for—both riches and honor—so that in your lifetime you will have no equal among kings'" (1 Kings 3:11-13).

Selah: God is still pleased with our prayer for discernment. Use Paul's prayer in Philippians 1:9-10 in praying for yourself and your family. *And this is my prayer: that your love may abound more + more in knowledge + depth of insight, so that you may be able to discern what is best + may be pure + blameless until the day of Christ*

7:5 Your head crowns you like Mount Carmel. Your hair is like royal tapestry; the king is held captive by its tresses.

The order of the description is interesting. The spiritually discerning nose mentioned in 7:4 must be first in order to recognize the presence of the enemy. Next, her head is described like "Carmel" to deal with the attack in the thought life where most of the trouble begins and plagues us! Carmel means vineyards or fruitful place. Her mind, under the control of the Holy Spirit, becomes a spiritual vineyard producing the needed fruit to dispel the enemy—thanksgiving in place of unthankful thoughts, love instead of hate, joy rather than sadness.

Mt. Carmel was considered one of the most excellent and beautiful peaks in the land. Her fruitful wisdom and purity of thought can now be compared to that Mount Carmel. Her hair, a symbol of consecration to God, is declared to have royal power that even holds the King captive.

Amazingly, when we surrender to Him, He "is held captive" and responds as though we are in charge. When we surrender, we are saying, "I will do whatever You choose." But to our surprise He replies, "You may ask me for anything in my name, and I will do it" (John 14:14).

Selah: Why can He give such an offer to those who yield Him complete control? They won't ask for anything contrary to His Name (to Him)

Lovingly Abandoned to Jesus

A heart that welcomes Jesus' leadership is the best thing the Spirit works in us. We then serve others for Jesus' sake, not just for our own sake or even primarily for the people's sake.

7:6 How beautiful you are and how pleasing, O love, with your delights!

Her loyal heart of abandoned love thrills Him. Her resolve to do His will, no matter what it costs her, fills her Bridegroom with delight and affection. He is completely captivated by His submissive, spiritually mature bride. Her love captures the King!

There are no more foxes to spoil the vines, no hidden compromise, and no unwillingness to arise when He calls her. She is as devoted to Him as He is to the Father.

He observes every detail concerning her and us also. He loves every little thing about us when we simply say, "Take it all," and mean it. Now we completely belong to

Him—our job, desires, mind, future, children, spouse— 👌
everything!

May He gaze upon each detail of our lives and say,
"How beautiful! How beautiful!"

Selah: What are three reasons our dedication to Jesus
gives Him great joy? *He sees our loyalty, our*
purity + our love that is Jesus centered not
self-centered

**7:7 Your stature is like that of the palm, and your breasts like
clusters of fruit.**

**7:8 I said, "I will go up to the palm tree, I will take hold of its
branches." Let now your breasts be like clusters of the vine,
The fragrance of your breath like apples, And the roof of your
mouth like the best wine. (NKJV)**

Her stature speaks of her maturity. Her attentiveness to
Him has made her like the palm tree, the emblem of
fruitfulness. The date palm was highly prized in biblical
times, and the fruit was valued more highly than bread
because of its sustaining power. One tree could yield up to
200 pounds of dates in a year, and its fruit bearing power
increased rather than decreased with age.

The more a palm tree is oppressed, the more it
flourishes. It will not be pressed or bound down or grow
crooked even if heavy weights are laid on it. He had never
described her this way before!

"The righteous will flourish like a palm tree...They will
still bear fruit in old age, they will stay fresh and
green" (Psalm 92: 12, 14).

He says he will take hold of its fruit. Her service would
be primarily for Him—even loving and caring for others.
In the Old Testament tabernacle, the bread was offered to
God for the first six days. After that, the priests could eat it.
When Jesus arose from the dead, He told Mary Magdalene
that He must first ascend to His Father. His death on the

cross was first of all for Him. All we do is first of all for Him and His pleasure.

Then He tells her three aspects of the ministry she will have. First, He promises that she will nurture others. Through her faith and love others will be cherished and spiritually matured. Breasts are mentioned eight times in the Song of Songs. Here, for the first time, they are likened to clusters of fruit. When we are totally His, we more easily abide in Him, and believe His promises so that we produce much fruit. He sees in her much fruit (John 15:5) as a result of her faith and love.

Second, through her the Holy Spirit will be released. In 2:3 she said, "With great delight I sat in his shadow, and his fruit was sweet to my taste." Here we discover the outcome of that communion. The apples she ate perfumed her breath, and now her life is permeated with the fragrance of His life. She is filled with the Holy Spirit whose name means "wind" or "breath" in the Hebrew, so the words she said had the fragrance of the anointing of the Spirit upon them.

Third, through it all, she will maintain her intimacy with Him. In the next verse, she speaks of her enthusiasm for what He has chosen for her.

Selah: When you do any act of kindness, offer it to Him first. When you do, He will receive it as though you did it just for Him. What kindness can you do for Him today?

Beloved

7:9 "The wine goes down smoothly for my beloved" (NKJV).

In love's poetic language, the statement that the wine goes down smoothly refers to her living in instantaneous agreement with the Holy Spirit's leadership. It goes down smoothly because she receives it without resistance drinking the cup of God's will without hindrance. "I delight to do Your will, O my God, and Your law is within my heart" (Psalm 40:8). No matter what happens, the spiritually mature can say, "The wine goes down smoothly because my Beloved loves me and I love Him."

"The wine goes down smoothly" is a phrase you can use when things come into your life that you might naturally resist. Because you love Jesus so much and want to please Him, your most loving response is, "The wine goes down smoothly. I say 'yes' to Your leadership and to what You allow."

She says, "May the wine..." She desires more than anything else to have a life that will never resist the Spirit. A heart that welcomes His leadership is the best thing the Spirit works in us. Still, delighting to do the will of God has a decision aspect to it. The more we choose to live in agreement with the Holy Spirit, the more He pours His love for Jesus into our hearts. The more we grieve Him by what we do with our eyes, speech, time, or money, the less we will love Jesus.

Wine is a symbol of joy. Not only does God bring us joy, but also we bring God joy. Jesus' most pleasurable thing outside of the Godhead is His love relationship with His Bride. Everything God does in a human heart is to glorify and satisfy Jesus. With bridal love in our hearts, we are able to love Jesus as He deserves to be loved. When we resist the Spirit, we are robbing Jesus of joy.

Selah: To what difficult situation can you apply these sentences? "I receive His will regarding _Family_ because I love Jesus and find my joy in pleasing Him. The wine goes down smoothly."

7:10 I belong to my lover, and his desire is for me.

Her Lover is overwhelmed with her beauty. He praises her qualities that describe her spiritual maturity. When He finishes, she gives Him the sweetest words a surrendered heart can say, "I belong to Him and His desire is for me."

This verse is the confession Jesus waits to hear from each of our hearts. His heart is moved when we say, "I belong to my Lover, and He desires me and I am committed to Him." The Message

"I belong to my lover." What she does is for Him. If others in the vineyard don't notice or appreciate what she did, that's insignificant. All she does is for Him.

"His desire is for me." Truly believing this truth—His desire is to do me good at all times in all ways—is the key to the walk of faith. It is also the underlying reason she can say, "His wine goes down smoothly." By living with this confidence, we can live the surrendered life consistently.

Being completely sure of His heart toward us changes us. We discover it is possible to give thanks in every kind of circumstance. Why? Because we know that even in the "bad" He is leading us through it, giving us strength, supplying every need, and always having a way to bring good out of all things (Philippians 4:4-6; 1 Thessalonians 5:18; Romans 8:28).

The Bride truly trusts His promises because she has deep insight into Jesus' affection and enjoyment of her. The most prominent theme in the Song is the revelation of God's desire for us. This revelation will powerfully change us. God's love for us and our love for Him become our primary motivation for obedience and diligence (Song 4:9; 6:4-5; 7:6-10). Insight into God's desire gives us spiritual and emotional security.

His heart is deeply moved by our steady love for Him. He even writes in His book about our tears (Psalm 56:8) and about our conversations about Him (Malachi 3:16). His thoughts about each of us cannot be numbered: He has

Record my lament; list my tears on your scroll, are they not in your record? Psalm 56:8

112

engraved our names on the palms of His hands (Psalm 139:17-18; Isaiah 49:16). Even when we have forgotten about Him, His desires and longings are for us.

Selah: Can you say with confidence, "I am absolutely convinced in my spirit that no matter what happens He has a good plan for me"? *Yes!*

Whenever you feel rejected by others or in difficult circumstances, try saying these words: "His desire is for me." What would be the impact of living with the reality of those words? *Peace*

Then those who feared the Lord talked w/ea. other + the Lord listened + heard. A scroll of remembrance was written in his presence concerning those who feared the Lord + honored his name.

Malachi 3:16

Poured Out Love

Our longings are met when we surrender unreservedly to Jesus. Instead of the cross we fear, we find the King of Love who satisfies our deepest longing and who finds His pleasure in us.

7:11 Come, my lover, let us go to the countryside, let us spend the night in the villages.

She is no longer working for those who forced her to take care of the vineyard (1:6). Her motivation now is her love for Him, for His love has compelled her (2 Corinthians 5:14). Our energy to serve springs from our confidence that Jesus deeply desires and loves us.

His passion draws her. He created within us a capacity for communion to which He could relate so He could have the fellowship and satisfaction He desires. Throughout Scripture, the Lord is revealed as a seeking God. He seeks for our fellowship.

She changed her language in Song 6:11 from "I went down" to "let us go." She uses "let us" four times (Song 7:11-12) indicating that they work together. A strong loving relationship results in mutual concerns. She now is interested in the harvest of the vineyard, too.

But she will not go without His presence. Her only concern is to be with Him in His work. She doesn't care what He asks her to do as long as He will release His presence as she goes.

Another version states, "Come, my beloved, let us go forth into the field" (KJV). Paul told the Corinthians, "For we are God's fellow workers; you are God's field" (1 Corinthians 3:9). Our "field" includes those we are with— our family, job, church, and neighborhood. It is where God places us. "Open your eyes and look at the fields! They are ripe for harvest" (John 4:35). Jesus is always concerned about those close to us.

To spend the night speaks of her diligence and urgency to carry out what He has assigned her.

Selah: What difference does it make when we think of what we do for God as though we are doing it with Him— not just for Him? Creates intimacy & union w/ J.C,

7:12 Let us go early to the vineyards to see if the vines have budded, if their blossoms have opened, and if the pomegranates are in bloom—there I will give you my love.

She is able to share His loving concern. No longer selfish, she is longing to bless others who once mistreated her. Her desire is to see others succeed. Sacrifice is no longer avoided. She will pay the price to touch others in His Name.

During her immature years, serving others became a distraction from her enjoyment of Him. Ministry was a hindrance. But now, ministry is where she gives Him her love.

It is in the good times but also in the disappointments, the setbacks, the seemingly fruitless times of ministry that we give Him our love. We serve for Jesus' sake, not just for the people's sake.

It was easy for her to love Jesus in chapter two, but as her maturity has deepened, she desires to express her love by being where the presence of Jesus will be released through all she does for Him.

Selah: Ask Jesus in what place of ministry you can give Him your love. *Show me Sweet Jesus, PLEASE!*

7:13 The mandrakes send out their fragrance, and at our door is every delicacy, both new and old, that I have stored up for you, my lover.

The mandrakes were considered a fruit symbolic of love and appeared in the fields at the time of wheat harvest. Harvest was a time of rejoicing and celebration, a time of praising God for His blessings. She was rejoicing because of her fruitful life that resulted from her union with Him. The fragrance of Jesus flowed from them as they labored in love together in the vineyard.

The doors represent the many and varied opportunities to serve. She is overjoyed to share with her Beloved all the blessings that going through the doors of opportunity have brought to her heart.

His door is her door so she calls it "our door." He chooses each door in which they will enter together. We are not to think of having "my" ministry, but if we are in union with Him, it is "our" ministry. Then "our" ministry will result in much fruit.

Selah: Ask Jesus to bring to your mind the many ways He has demonstrated His love to you in both the past and the present.

8:1 If only you were to me like a brother, who was nursed at my mother's breasts! Then, if I found you outside, I would kiss you, and no one would despise me.

The maiden longs to boldly show her loyalty and affection to her Lover in public. A woman at that time in history could be more "familiar in public" with her brother than her fiancé.

To "kiss Jesus in public" without being despised speaks of expressing the fullness of our heart to Him in public without being misunderstood and looked down upon. Peter and John prayed for this boldness. "Now, Lord, consider their threats and enable your servants to speak your word with great boldness" (Acts 4:29).

Selah: In what situations is speaking boldly for Jesus most difficult? *w/ Non believers*

When has God helped you have a public witness to your faith? *Always it is Him that enables + get the glory I do nothing on my own that is fruitful*

8:2 I would lead you and bring you to my mother's house—she who has taught me. I would give you spiced wine to drink, the nectar of my pomegranates.

She longs to bring His presence to those in the Church, her mother's house. This speaks of those who initially taught her the things of God. (Paul spoke in Galatians 4:26 of the New Jerusalem as "the mother of us all," so the mother is considered to be symbolic of the Church.)

It is easy to hold back when we are with familiar relationships. A prophet is often not received in his hometown. "Jesus said to them, 'Only in his hometown and in his own house is a prophet without honor'" (Matthew 13:57). But she is willing to minister to those who knew her when she was just starting to walk with God. She would share with young and old what it means to give your life over in total abandonment to Christ.

There in her mother's house she wants to serve Him with the best she has. Pomegranates were expensive, but she would treat Him as her honored guest, no matter what it cost her.

She prays, "I would lead You." Jesus allows us to make some of the decisions in His kingdom. He gives us authority and He cooperates with our decisions. This reveals the dignity He has given us as co-heirs with Him. "We are heirs—heirs of God and co-heirs with Christ" (Romans 8:17).

Selah: Why do you think the maiden found it difficult to speak boldly of what she had learned to those who knew her best?

Is it difficult for you to speak openly of the way Jesus is leading you when you are at your church, in your home, or with your friends? If so, why? What steps can you take to overcome this? yes. Trust in Him + yield to Him

8:3 His left arm is under my head and his right arm embraces me.

8:4 Daughters of Jerusalem, I charge you: Do not arouse or awaken love until it so desires.

Her source of strength and support is her Bridegroom's embrace. His left arm supported her head, directing her thoughts. His right arm embraced her, supplying strength. He was her resting place. "The eternal God is your refuge, and underneath are the everlasting arms" (Deut. 33:27).

There is nothing sweeter to the Bridegroom or to the bride than this hallowed and unhindered communion. No one was to disturb her in this moment of glory with the King.

This time the phrase "Do not arouse or awaken love..." is given, the easily frightened gazelles are omitted because her days of fear and timidity are over. She is caught up with Him and not so easily disturbed.

Each time He has caused her to rest in His love He was preparing her for a new spiritual step. It is the same now. He knows she will need strength that comes from His love for this journey. So He takes her into His arms. Falling into His embrace is a complete surrender to His strength.

Selah: Why is our time alone with God the most important preparation we can make for all that lies ahead?

He is our source
He is life
we must remain in Him
we must abide in His Love

Friends

8:5 Who is this coming up from the wilderness, Leaning upon her beloved? NKJV

Perhaps her Beloved allowed her to go through a "wilderness experience" so she would understand her need to totally depend upon Him. To bring us to entire reliance and dependence upon Him is His purpose for what He allows in our lives.

Her friends see her now leaning upon her Beloved, for she has learned that she can only keep in step with Him as she leans upon Him each moment in complete dependence.

Others can tell if we are leaning on Jesus or if we are depending on our own strength. For instance, are we leaning on Him to change those we care about or are we trying to convince them with our own efforts? The bride's friends took notice that she rested completely, moving only when He moved and stopping only when He stopped.

He is her strength, joy, and pride, while she is His treasure, the object of His most tender care. All His resources of wisdom and strength are hers. By leaning and having no confidence in self, she has discovered an endless source of strength in Him.

Selah: Have you ever gone through a difficult time that caused you to depend entirely on Him?

Lover

I awakened you under the apple tree. There your mother brought you forth; There she who bore you brought you forth. (NKJV)

Again, He reminds her that He is more than a Bridegroom to her. Before she knew Him, He knew her, and of this He reminds her. He called her to Himself when she had no attraction. The love that made her what she is, and now takes delight in her, is not a fickle love. She does not need to fear it will change.

The apple tree is a picture of Christ in the beauty of His love. Under the shadow of His love, He lavishes His affection on us by giving us a desire for Him. Then the intercessions of the Church bring us to new birth in Christ.

Selah: How did the Savior show you His love before you had a desire for Him? *He saved me from evil when I cried out to him.*

8:6 Place me like a seal over your heart, like a seal on your arm; for love is as strong as death, its jealousy unyielding as the grave. It burns like blazing fire, like a mighty flame.

The Bridegroom is calling His maiden to set Him as a seal on her heart. This seal declares that she belongs to Him. He "set his seal of ownership on us, and put his Spirit in our hearts" (2 Corinthians 1:22).

The "heart" is the place of love, and He wants all of our love to be for Him. He is saying, "Set Me as a seal upon your affections; let them all be directed toward Me."

The "arm" represents our activities. His seal of ownership on us demands that none of our actions grieve the Holy Spirit. Every deed, every activity must have His approval.

The seal of the Holy Spirit is the infilling of God's love poured into our hearts. "God has poured out his love into our hearts by the Holy Spirit, whom he has given us" (Romans 5:5). As He pours out His love into our hearts, we will be filled with a passion that can be described as a blazing fire. We will be passionate about what He is passionate about. We will be enabled to love as He loves.

We must invite Him to place His seal of love on us. He will not force us into a relationship of intimate love. In response to our asking with faith, He will set His seal of ownership on us so that we will spend our strength and our energies only for Him and His Kingdom.

Jesus is a jealous Lover. He will not relent until we love Him with all of our hearts. The love that "is as strong as death" led Him to His death on the cross. Now He yearns for us to love Him as He loves us.

His jealousy over us is "unyielding as the grave." "The LORD, whose name is Jealous, is a jealous God" (Exodus 34:14). He cannot overlook one spot or wrinkle in His bride. He is asking us to choose to have every desire, decision and circumstance filtered through the crucified One. We ask, "Would You be pleased for me to spend my time like this? Would You be pleased to watch this with me? Would it please You for me to wear this? Would You be pleased for me to buy this?" The crucified life is living with the total confidence that He knows best and we delight in His choices.

This is good!!

Jesus asks for a total commitment from us. He is not content with a partial ownership of our hearts. May we be fiercely protective of God's claims on our lives and allow nothing to steal what belongs to Him—our time, money, interest.

Jesus has an intense jealousy toward anything that would come between Him and His Bride. He sets before us the vision, the commitment that it will take, and the path we must walk. "And do not grieve the Holy Spirit of God, with whom you were sealed for the day of redemption" (Ephesians 4:30).

The phrase "for love is strong as death..." is speaking of Divine love. Divine love gives us victory to overcome temptations that we could not overcome with human efforts. But when our source of strength comes from Divine love, we can endure anything. Millions of martyrs have loved Jesus with that strength.

Selah: Are you living the crucified life? "The crucified life is living with the total confidence that He knows best and we delight in His choices."

8:7 Many waters cannot quench love, nor can the floods drown it. If a man would give for love all the wealth of his house, it would be utterly despised. (NKJV)

Nothing can put out the flame of love. "Many waters" and "floods" signify trials that believers go through. Rivers of persecution, misunderstanding, heartache, disappointments or pain cannot quench Divine love. The enemy will send the waters of temptation, apathy, disappointment, or pain to put this fire out. But when we continually yield to the Spirit, He constantly pours love into our hearts.

Once we have met our beloved Jesus and are filled with His love, the highest temptation that this world offers us—money, position or fame—pales by comparison.

Selah: Is there anything that keeps you from being totally committed to Jesus? If not, ask the Holy Spirit to put His seal of ownership in your heart. You may want to write to Jesus your commitment to give Him all of Yourself so you can receive all of Him. "...to you who believe, He is precious" (1 Peter 2:7 NKJV).

The Seal of Love

Now that she has the seal of His love in her heart (Song 8:6-7), the Bride is aware of the spiritual condition of others. She doesn't seek to meet their needs on her own but looks to Jesus for guidance.

Beloved

8:8 We have a young sister, and her breasts are not yet grown. What shall we do for our sister for the day she is spoken for?

Once Jesus sets the seal of fiery love in her heart (Song 8:6-7), the Bride turns her attention away from her own spiritual condition to that of the needs of others. The fact that she even "sees" her sister's need is the work of the Spirit in her.

She feels the same towards the little sister as Jesus does. He is ravished over her (4:9) and longs to see her face and hear her voice (2:14). She recognizes that this immature believer is her responsibility, and she is burdened for her.

The word "young" also means "little." This sister is little in faith and so easily loses her courage in difficulties. She quickly gives up in pressure. Her breasts are not yet grown, so she is unable to nurture others with the milk of the Word. She fellowships with those she hangs out with but neglects to take responsibility for others. She is overwhelmed with her own problems. The Bride wants to help, so she intercedes for her. Now that the seal of love is on her heart, she is compelled by that love to be concerned for others. (2 Corinthians 5:14)

The Bride says, "We have a young sister," because she is working closely with Him. She does not say, "What will 'I' do for my sister," but rather, "What will we do," indicating that she is in partnership with Jesus. She is burdened for others and feels the same concern He feels.

"What shall we do?" She will not make her plans and then ask for His blessing but will learn what His thoughts are and together they will fulfill His plans. We would be spared much anxiety if we always sought to know His thoughts. When we let Him lead us and leave the responsibility with Him, our strength is not exhausted with worry and we accomplish His purposes.

Selah! Why is it easy to lose a sincere interest in others' spiritual growth? What are ways we can increase our concern? 1) When we forget it is His work + not ours + then get frustrated when they don't respond as quickly as we'd like. 2) Ask to see w/ his eyes

Lover

8:9 If she is a wall, we will build towers of silver on her. If she is a door, we will enclose her with panels of cedar.

The Bridegroom sweetly responds acknowledging His oneness with her. "We will build...we will enclose." He will not do His work without her but will work with and through her. What is done for this sister, however, will depend upon where she is in relation to Him. The bride would need discernment; not everyone needs the same help to mature spiritually.

"If she is a wall" speaks of one who is mature enough to defend herself from spiritual enemies. Cities with walls were well defended, but cities without walls were defenseless. Spiritual towers will allow her to see the enemy's tactics. Silver represents redemption. He and the Bride will teach her to reach others with a redemptive purpose, so she can bring others to salvation.

But if the sister is unstable and easily moved like a door, she will need to be enclosed with boards of cedar. Cedar was an especially strong wood with a pleasing fragrance. It was not likely to decay so was used for building and adorning temples and royal palaces. He will work through His bride to strengthen the sister who is immature.

This will happen when the bride begins to pray specific promises from the Word doing spiritual warfare over her sister. The bride will spend time just being a friend to her little sister so she can see what a mature Christian really is. She will bear her burdens and give her words of hope and encouragement.

We must realize that our every move is being observed. That is how the little sisters are taught. They must see the Christian life lived out—a walk of humility, patience, caring and accountability. And they must be supported by our prayers and encouraged through the Word.

Selah: What "little sister" might God be asking you to help grow deeper in her faith? What are ways you might accomplish this? How are you allowing her to see the victorious Christian life lived out?

Sharing Struggles + triumphs

126

8:10 I am a wall, and my breasts are like towers. Thus I have become in his eyes like one bringing contentment.

A remarkable confidence now fills her heart. She acknowledges that she is mature and able to protect and bless others. Her breasts like towers speak of her great ability to nurture and give sustenance to many.

She has become one who has grown to a place of maturity, bringing great contentment to Jesus. His heart has longed for His flock to be cared for and protected. Without boasting she could describe her progress as Paul did: "Follow my example, as I follow the example of Christ" (1 Corinthians 11:1). Jesus wants to bring each of us to the place where we know we satisfy Him and that He has pleasure in us.

The maiden had this confidence because she had a witness in her heart that she was doing the will of God. We expend much emotional energy when we condemn ourselves and live with self-doubt and uncertainty. He wants us to enjoy a radiant confidence that we are living with pure motives and serving Jesus with all our hearts. This is gloriously possible after He has put His seal on us by pouring His passionate love into our hearts by the Holy Spirit.

Selah: Despite our failures, we can live with a desire to please Him and believe that our desire gives Him pleasure. Why does it please Jesus for us to think of ourselves as bringing Him contentment? *We are wholeheartedly devoted to Him. we have an undivided heart for Him*

8:11 Solomon had a vineyard in Baal Hamon; he let out his vineyard to tenants. Each one was to bring for its fruit a thousand shekels of silver.

8:12 But my own vineyard is mine to give; the thousand shekels are for you, O Solomon, and two hundred are for those who tend its fruit.

"Baal Hamon" means "place of a multitude." Jesus has many servants, and just as Solomon leased his vineyard, Jesus entrusted the responsibility of His vineyard to a multitude of tenants (Matthew 21:33). He gives each of us a certain area of His vineyard to tend for Him.

She knows that each one will give an account one day to the King for her assignment (Luke 12:31-48). "Each of us will give an account of himself to God" (Romans 14:12). "For we must all appear before the judgment seat of Christ, that each one may receive what is due him for the things done while in the body, whether good or bad" (2 Corinthians 5:10).

Silver represents redemption, so the fruit He expects will be works for the purpose of seeing souls redeemed. Each must bring a thousand pieces of silver. The "thousand" is a complete number that speaks of the full measure that God requires according to what was entrusted to each person.

The Bride says before her Bridegroom, "I am ready to give account to You because I have given You the thousand that You asked for." She has given all He expected from her. In 1:6 she was made a keeper of vineyards though she neglected her own. Now after becoming His beloved Bride, her own vineyard is full and mature, bearing magnificent fruit.

Her vineyard was a way she could give to Him. All we do is always to be our personal expression of love to Jesus. His reward is enough. As Oswald Chambers said, "If you are devoted to the cause of humanity, you will soon be exhausted...but if the <u>mainspring of your service is love for</u> <u>Jesus, you can serve men though they treat you like a</u> <u>doormat."</u>

She acknowledges that those who "keep its fruit," or her fellow workers, will have a portion in her fruitfulness when they stand before God. She fulfilled her calling as she worked in team relationship with others. Many helped her in her vineyard. Each worker on the team will share in her reward in eternity. The 200 shekels of silver speak of the portion of reward that her co-workers will receive on the last day.

Selah: "God is not unjust; he will not forget your work and the love you have shown him as you have helped his people" (Hebrews 6:10). What do you think your response will be on the day God hands out rewards in heaven? Do you believe you are giving Him the full measure He expects?

Lover

8:13 You who dwell in the gardens with friends in attendance, let me hear your voice!

The journey ends with a happy exchange of love between the maiden and her Bridegroom. He affirms her as one who is still dwelling in the midst of God's garden serving His people. He speaks of companions. Jesus loves to have us speak with others about Him. He even has an angel taking notes! "Then those whose lives honored God got together and talked it over. God saw what they were doing and listened in. A book was opened in God's presence and minutes were taken of the meeting, with the names of the God-fearers written down, all the names of those who honored God's name" (Malachi 3:16 The Message). Her companions eagerly listen for her voice because they recognize and appreciate her wisdom.

He has a final desire filling His heart, "Let Me hear your voice..." He longs to hear her voice in worship and intercession as well as teaching and evangelism. We satisfy His longing when we pray. Every time we whisper, "I love You, Lord," we are bringing the most precious sound to His ears. Our cry for revival is a love song to Jesus.

Jesus appreciates our good deeds, our witnessing, our teaching a Bible class, but if those activities crowd out our time alone with Him, He misses us and feels neglected.

His final words caution us to never allow busyness, offenses, tensions and pressures drown out our daily devotion to minister to His heart.

Selah: How does knowing your time with God immensely pleases Him change the way you view your daily devotions? *It is mutually beneficial — not just one sided*

Beloved

8:14 Come away, my lover, and be like a gazelle or like a young stag on the spice-laden mountains.

The Song ends showing that her prayer in 1:4 to be drawn to her Beloved has been answered. Now she is leaping and running with Him. She is echoing the very words He once spoke to draw her to the mountains. She desires for Him to steal away and run with her.

In 2:17, she had asked her Lover to turn and go without her to the "rugged hills." Now that she has tasted the pure joy of His love, she is eager to go with Him.

In 4:6, she willingly chose to go with Him to the mountain of myrrh, a place that she knew would involve sacrifice.

But now, she recognizes there will be mountains ahead, but she does not care! Her journey with Jesus will be filled with sweet joys because the mountains will be fragrant with His presence. The bride has discovered the indescribable joy of being loved by the King whose love knows no bounds. She does not fear the journey ahead for it will be through "spice-laden mountains."

When we learn the sweetness of communion with Jesus and the joys of receiving His love, our fears melt away in anticipation of a life He lovingly chooses for us.

Selah: The maiden's journey from being merely a worker for Jesus to being a lover of Jesus started with a desire to be kissed by His Word. Do you know the joy of allowing Jesus to cherish you by receiving His love through Scripture? *Yes! Hallelujah! Praise You, Jesus!!*

Appendix A:
Voices from the Past

"Should we interpret Song of Songs as addressing our relationship with God in nuptial terms?

World Editor Marvin Olasky affirms that Scripture speaks repeatedly and explicitly in the Song of Songs and in the prophets about our relationship with God in sexual terms. Below are statements he quotes from Puritan writers as well as Spurgeon, Tozer, and others.

John Cotton of First Church in Boston, describing how we should long for Christ, wrote, "It will inflame our hearts to kisse him again."

Timothy Keller stated: "Sex is for fully committed relationships because it is to be a foretaste of the joy that comes from being in complete union with God. The most rapturous love between a man and woman is only a hint of God's love for us (Romans 7:1–6; Ephesians 5:21–33)...We are called to experience the spousal love of Jesus."

John Piper said Hosea 2:14-23 is one of the "tenderest and most beautiful love songs in the Bible...But the most daring statement of all is the last one in verse 20: 'And you shall know the Lord.' To see what this means recall the peculiar use of the word 'know' in the Bible. For example, Genesis 4:1, 'Adam knew Eve his wife and she conceived and bore Cain.' And Matthew 1:25, 'Joseph knew her [Mary] not until she had borne a son.'"

John Calvin stated, "The strong affection which a husband ought to cherish towards his wife is exemplified by Christ, and an instance of that unity which belongs to marriage is declared to exist between himself and the Church. This is a remarkable passage on the mysterious intercourse which we have with Christ."

In *Institutes of Christian Religion*, Calvin wrote, "God very commonly takes on the character of a husband to us. Indeed, the union by which he binds us to himself when he receives us into the bosom of the church is like sacred wedlock..."

Thomas Shepard, whose writings profoundly shaped Jonathan Edwards, preached, "Consider he makes love to thee. Not one soul that hears me this day but the Lord Jesus is a suitor unto, that now ye would be espoused to him; He came unto his own, and they received him not."

A.W. Tozer in *The Pursuit of God* wrote, "The continuous and unembarrassed interchange of love and thought between God and the soul of the redeemed man is the throbbing heart of New Testament religion. This intercourse between God and the soul is known to us in conscious personal awareness."

You can read more of these quotes at http://www.aholyexperience.com/intimacy-with-God.

Scriptures on this holy mystical union:

"As a bridegroom rejoices over his bride, so will your God rejoice over you" (Isaiah 62:5).

"I betrothed you to one husband, to present you as a pure virgin to Christ" (2 Corinthians 11:2 ESV).

"For your Maker is your husband—the LORD Almighty is his name" (Isaiah 54:5).

"Therefore, behold, I will allure her, and bring her into the wilderness, and speak tenderly to her...And in that day, declares the LORD, you will call me 'My Husband,' and no longer will you call me 'My Baal.'...And I will betroth you to me forever. I will betroth you to me in righteousness and in justice, in steadfast love and in mercy...I will betroth you to me in faithfulness. And you shall know the LORD" (Hosea 2:14, 16, 19, 20 ESV).

"That they all may be one, as thou Father are in me, and I in thee, that they may be one in us" (John 17:21 KJV).

"I gave you my solemn oath and entered into a covenant with you, declares the Sovereign LORD, and you became mine. Then I bathed you with water, washed off your blood from you and anointed you with oil... 'I bathed you with water and washed the blood from you and put ointments on you. I clothed you with an embroidered dress and put sandals of fine leather on you. I dressed you in fine linen and covered you with costly garments...You adulteress wife, you prefer strangers to your own husband!" (Ezekiel 16:8-10, 32).

Appendix B:
Scriptures for Worship

Praise Verses

If we truly praise God, He will fulfill His promise to do what He says in Psalm 50:23: "He who sacrifices thank offerings honors me, and he prepares the way so that I may show him the salvation of God." Your praising God prepares a path for His deliverance.

"Who among the gods is like you, O LORD? Who is like you—majestic in holiness, awesome in glory, working wonders?" (Exodus 15:11).

"He is the Rock, his works are perfect, and all his ways are just. A faithful God who does no wrong, upright and just is he" (Deuteronomy 32:4).

"Praise be to you, Lord, the God of our father Israel, from everlasting to everlasting. Yours, Lord, is the greatness and the power and the glory and the majesty and the splendor, for everything in heaven and earth is yours.

"Yours, Lord, is the kingdom; you are exalted as head over all. Wealth and honor come from you; you are the ruler of all things. In your hands are strength and power to exalt and give strength to all.

"Now, our God, we give you thanks, and praise your glorious name." (2 Chronicles 29:10-13).

"I will exalt you, my God the King; I will praise your name for ever and ever. Every day I will praise you and extol your name for ever and ever.

"Great is the Lord and most worthy of praise; his greatness no one can fathom" (Psalm 145:1-3).

"O LORD, God of our fathers, are you not the God who is in heaven? You rule over all the kingdoms of the nations. Power and might are in your hand, and no one can withstand you" (2 Chronicles 20:6).

"I will extol the LORD at all times; his praise will always be on my lips. My soul will boast in the LORD; let the afflicted hear and rejoice. Glorify the LORD with me; let us exalt his name together. Taste and see that the LORD is good; blessed is the man who takes refuge in him. Fear the LORD, you his saints, for those who fear him lack nothing" (Psalm 34:1-3, 8-9).

"Enter his gates with thanksgiving and his courts with praise; give thanks to him and praise his name" (Psalm 100:4).

"Praise the Lord, O my soul; all my inmost being, praise his holy name" (Psalm 103:1).

"Not to us, O Lord, not to us but to your name be the glory, because of your love and faithfulness" (Psalm 115:1).

Prayers Adapted from Scripture

"Take the helmet of salvation and the sword of the Spirit, which is the word of God. And pray in the Spirit" (Ephesians 6:17-19). The implication is that we are to take the Word of God with us when we expect to pray in the Spirit. God loves to hear us bring His Word to Him in prayer.

- Give _____ this day her daily bread (Matthew 6:11).
- Deliver _____ from the evil one (Matthew 6:13).
- Help _____ to be joyful always; pray continually, and to give thanks in all circumstances recognizing that this is God's will for her in Christ Jesus (1 Thessalonians 5:15-18).
- Help _____ to never tire of doing what is right (2 Thessalonians 3:13).
- May _____ experience the love of Christ, though it is so great she will never fully understand it (Ephesians 3:19).
- Help _____ not to rely on herself but on God (2 Corinthians 1:9).
- Equip _____ with everything good for doing Your will and work in her what is pleasing to you (Hebrews 13:21).
- Fill _____ with the knowledge of your will through all spiritual wisdom and understanding (Colossians 1:9).
- Direct _____ heart into God's love and Christ's perseverance (2 Thessalonians 3:5).
- I pray that _____ may prosper in all things and be in health, just as her soul prospers (3 John 1:2).
- Help _____ to be joyful always; pray continually, and to give thanks in all circumstances recognizing that this is God's will for him in Christ Jesus (1 Thessalonians 5:16-18).
- Make all grace abound to _____, so that in all things at all times, having all that he needs, he will abound in every good work (2 Corinthians 9:8).

- I pray that out of Your glorious riches, You would strengthen _____ with power through Your Spirit in his inner being, so that Christ may dwell in his heart through faith (Ephesians 3:16).

- I pray that _____ love may abound more and more in knowledge and depth of insight, so that she may be able to discern what is best and may be pure and blameless until the day of Christ (Philippians 1:10).

Appendix C:
Names and Descriptions of God

Abiding, Absolute, Anointed, Atonement, All in All, Almighty, All-powerful, Attorney, All-sufficient

Benevolent, Blessed, Believing, Benefactor, Bread, Branch, Beautiful, Beloved, Beginning

Compassionate, Caring, Creative, Christ, Counselor, Comforter, Creator, Corrector, Cornerstone, Captain, Companion, Carpenter

Determined, Divine, Dear, Devoted, Deliverer, Defender, Door, Dove, Dayspring, Daystar

Everlasting, Eternal, Encourager, Everything, End, Emancipator, Example, El Shaddai

Forgiving, Faithful, Father, Friend, Foundation, Fountain, Finisher, Fortress

Glorious, Good, Gentle, Guileless, God, Gate, Grace, Guide, Giver, Gracious, Generous, Guardian

Holy, Humble, Hopeful, Holy Spirit, Helper, Head, Holy One, Hope, High Priest, Healer

Immortal, Invisible, Indestructible, Intercessor, Immanuel, Instructor, Incarnate, Infinite, Impartial, Incarnation, Invincible, Incorruptible, Inspirer

Just, Jealous, Jesus, Judge, Jehovah

Kind, Knowing, King of Kings

Loving, Lasting, Lord of Lords, Lord of Hosts, Life, Light, Lion of Judah, Lamb of God, Lover,

Merciful, Mighty, Majestic, Messiah, Master, Maker, Mighty One, Miraculous, Meek, Matchless,

Nobel, Nourishing

Omniscient, Omnipresent, Omega, Omnipotent

Powerful, Pure, Priest, Prince of Peace, Prophet, Persistent, Perfect, Power, Protector, Paraclete

Righteous, Restorer, Resting Place, Redeemer, Ruler, Rock, Refuge, Regenerator, Resurrection, Revelation, Rewarder

Sovereign, Sincere, Strong, Salvation, Shepherd, Self-Existent, Son of God, Sustainer, Sanctifier

Tolerant, Tactful, Teacher, Truth

Understanding, Unchanging, Unfathomable

Victorious, Vine, Victor

Wise, Wonderful, Wisdom, Way, Watchman

Yearning, Yahweh

Zealous

Appendix D:
Women Role Models

My Praying Mother

By Wesley Duewel

Psalm 126:5-6 gives the basis for my remarks about my godly mother: "Those who sow in tears will reap with songs of joy. He who goes out weeping, carrying seed to sow, will return with songs of joy, carrying sheaves with him."

On my mother's tombstone are the dates of her birth and death and one word, "Intercessor." Prayer was Mother's life.

She had a godly mother who prayed. One of the things that kept convicting my mother of her need of sanctification was going near the upstairs steps and hearing her mother on her knees weeping and praying that

God would deliver her daughter Ida from her terrible temper. I never saw that temper, because God delivered her.

My mother went to a minister and said, "I read these wonderful things in the book of Acts that God did in the early church. How can I have this experience?"

The minister said, "Oh, that's not for you. That was just for the apostles back there."

Mother was so distressed, but she soon received a letter from a sister saying, "I have just been filled with the Spirit!"

"Filled with the Spirit!" my mother exclaimed. That's what I want! My sister's been filled with the Spirit! Lord, I'll not go to sleep tonight until I know that I, too, am filled with the Spirit."

She worked hard all day as a helper in the home of her older sister whose husband was the minister she had questioned, and so when night came she was tired. However, she went to bed determined to pray all night if necessary. She was so weary she went to sleep, though, and in the morning she cried, "Oh, Lord, how can you sanctify me? How can you fill me with the Spirit if I'm so lazy as that?"

Again, she worked hard all day, washing clothes, taking care of the little children, and doing all the things she had to do, but that night she stated, "Lord, tonight I am not going to sleep until I know I'm filled with the Spirit." Once again she went to sleep in spite of her best intention.

The next morning, though, while lighting the fire, she sang in German a little song, "Into my heart, into my heart, come into my heart, Lord Jesus." Suddenly her faith took hold of God's promise, and she was filled with the Spirit.

So I, from my earliest memories, knew a Spirit-filled, praying mother.

Jesus saved me when I was five years old. Mother was putting me to bed and praying with me, and I exclaimed, "Mommy, don't stop praying. It's doing me so much good!" She prayed on, and while she prayed, she later told me, I jumped off the bed to the floor and hopped around crying, "Oh, Mommy, Mommy, Jesus just came into my heart!" So it was my mother's prayers that helped bring me into the kingdom.

It wasn't long after that that God called me to India. We had no missionary meeting in progress; my parents never knew why the call came at that time and in that way, although they prayed for many countries in the world. I came running into the house from the sandbox, crying, "Oh, Mommy, Mommy, Jesus just told me when I get big I'm supposed to go to India to tell people about him. Mommy, I want you to go along with me!"

And she did, in her prayers—two and three hours a day.

My earliest clear memory as a child is my mother placing her chair in the middle of the kitchen floor every morning. I would get my little red chair and pull it up beside her chair, and when mother kneeled down and prayed, I, too, would kneel by my little red chair beside Mother.

Mother prayed as she worked. She prayed as she washed clothes. She prayed as she washed dishes. While washing dishes and praying one day, she suddenly heard heavenly music coming as if from the sky outside the kitchen window. She later told me, "The next thing I knew, I was standing just looking up and listening to that beautiful heavenly music."

Mother prayed for the people in our church. She prayed for the people in the community. She prayed for unsaved loved ones and friends. However, there were two great burdens on Mother's heart. I cannot remember a family prayer time in the last thirty years of her life when I

144

was home from God's Bible School or when I was home from the mission field but that Mother would pray for China and for India. And I cannot remember one time when she prayed for China and India without weeping.

I'm here today in God's service because several times in my life God touched me while people were praying. One of those people who prayed for me was my mother. At the close of World War II while living in India, I got a cablegram from the United States saying that a missionary family was arriving on a ship in Calcutta. I was to meet them. At that time in India, authorities were not allowed to announce the arrival or departure of ships, so I did not know when the ship was coming.

I got on the train within a couple of hours of the cablegram. After arriving in Calcutta, I got off the train and was walking down the street to the American Express Company to get information about ships when a riot broke out just in front of me. There were more than 350 to 400 people killed on the streets of Calcutta during those next four or five days, and I had to make numerous trips through mobs where people were shouting right and left, waving their fists, and waving hockey sticks. I would push through that crowd, walking slowly, and the people would just keep parting. I felt that I could touch God if I moved my arm out eight to ten inches. I was surrounded by God.

About a week or two later, I received a letter from my mother saying, "Wesley, were you in any special danger on such and such days?"

Yes, those were the days I was in mob danger in Calcutta. She didn't know I was in Calcutta. My missionary society didn't know I was in Calcutta. Most of my missionaries didn't know I was in Calcutta. However, God knew, and God alerted mother. Her SOS prayers were what God used, and I'm here today thanking God for those prayers.

Mother was wonderfully healed after four years of serious illness, and thereafter, God used Mother's prayers for the healing of people in special ways. Many times people would call my parents before they called the doctor because they wanted someone to pray.

I came home from high school one day and Mother said, "Oh, Wesley, God has been so good to us today. Sister Gregg scalded her hand, but Jesus healed her." At Mother's memorial service, I learned the details of that incident. Sister Gregg told how she was in the kitchen and had spilled boiling syrup on her hand. The skin and flesh peeled back and just hung down. She was able to get hold of the central operator on the country phone and told the operator to call my parents who came immediately. When my father and mother walked in the door, my mother saw the hand and said, "Oh, Sister Gregg—" and Mother touched her hand. "Instantly," said Sister Gregg, "my hand was healed without a mark or a scar that I'd ever been scalded."

We were in Humboldt, Nebraska, and one of our parishioners, Brother Koontz, came down with appendicitis. The doctor was called and said, "I'll get an ambulance and rush you to the hospital." However, by that time the Koontzs had called my parents, and we arrived at the house before the ambulance. We went inside and began to pray, and God healed Brother Koontz. A few minutes later, the doctor came rushing in with the ambulance attendants. Bro. Koontz met them at the door with a big smile and said, "Praise the Lord, doctor, you came too late. The Lord beat you! I'm already healed!"

Brother Koontz never had another attack of appendicitis.

My mother's prayers still live on. During the past twelve or thirteen years, the world's greatest harvest in missions has occurred inside mainland China. There were approximately 900,000 Protestants in China before Mao, but since Mao's death, Christianity has flourished. The most conservative estimates today say that there are between 50 million and 60 million believers in China. Some even estimate there to be 75 million to 100 million believers. As I've heard this, I've often thought of Mother's tears for China. She who wept with tears, day after day, now has the joy of seeing the harvest.

To God be all the glory!

Dr. Wesley Duewel, past president of OMS International and author of several dynamic books on prayer including *Ablaze for God* and *Mighty Prevailing Prayer,* gave these remarks in a Women Alive meeting in Dayton, Ohio.

One Life Committed to Jesus
By Cricket Albertson
(Granddaughter of Elsie Kinlaw)

Sixty-four years ago, a lovely, slender girl made her way to Asbury College in Wilmore, Kentucky, from Schenectady, New York, for her first semester of college. She had no idea how dramatically her life would change during her time at Asbury.

Elsie Blake went to Asbury College because it had a pretty name and because her father thought it was a Christian school. Within two weeks of Elsie's freshman year, Asbury held a fall revival. At that revival Elsie met the Lord Jesus. Walking back to her dorm, she said that the presence of Jesus was so real that she felt His physical reality by her side. And that feeling lasted her whole life— a month before she went to heaven, Elsie said, "I have never been able to get away from what Jesus did for me that day in Hughes Auditorium."

Several weeks after meeting Jesus, Elsie was bouncing down her dormitory stairs, and looked out a window. At that moment, she heard Jesus whisper, "You have given me your heart; would you give me your whole life?" Her answer to Him characterized every other answer she would ever give to Him: "Oh, Jesus, Yes!"

After that, Elsie's life was marked by a passionate love for Jesus, for people, and for service. Those commitments that Elsie made to Jesus determined every other decision she made, and became the cornerstone for all that Jesus would do with her life.

One of the most impressive achievements to me, her granddaughter, was how she kept her first love. I think she had three ways to maintain her love relationship with Jesus Christ.

First, she sought His presence. She found delight in spending time with Him, and she insisted on that time. If she had any spare moments, she would go into a quiet corner and begin to talk to Jesus. He was her relaxation and her strength.

Second, she listened to the Holy Spirit's voice. When He whispered to her heart, she immediately obeyed. As a result of this listening heart, she chose to separate herself from anything that contained a taint of sin. For instance, when she was a young bride, she was staying with her family while her new husband was preaching. She said that she heard the Holy Spirit whisper to her not to spend her evenings watching TV, so when her family watched television she would sneak upstairs, work on a scrapbook, and pray for her new husband who was out telling people about Jesus.

In decisions like this, apparently small decisions, the pattern of her life was set. Not recreation first, not Elsie first, not family first, but Jesus first. The rest of her life, she consistently prayed through the hours when her husband was preaching. She had established her choice of Jesus first long before. She was willing to live without anything as long as she had Jesus.

Finally, she never let anything come between her and her first love. If she felt she had offended Christ in any way, she immediately asked for His forgiveness. She was even free to ask for others' forgiveness if she felt she had spoken in haste! She lived her life with a clean heart and with a passionate commitment to let the Holy Spirit keep it clean.

Not long after Elsie Blake fell in love with Jesus, she gave her testimony at a prayer meeting. One man in the audience listened with more than a casual interest. Dennis Kinlaw knew that he wanted to marry a girl who loved Jesus as Elsie Blake did. They began dating, and Elsie fell in love with Dennis the way she had fallen in love with the Lord Jesus—completely, unconditionally, and forever. The love story of Dennis and Elsie Kinlaw is a testimony to the faithful, passionate, and devoted love that is possible between a husband and wife. One morning I entered their home while Elsie was saying good-bye to my grandfather. It was a rather subdued parting; I think she kissed his cheek. When they saw me, she smiled and said, "When we get to heaven, we're going to spend the first five hundred years kissing." Fifty-nine years later and she was as in love with Dennis as on the day she became his bride.

But their love testifies to more. It symbolizes the passionate and faithful love that is possible between Christ and His church. The purity and faithfulness of their love came because of their commitment to Jesus first. Elsie's life verse became Matthew 6:33: "Seek ye first the kingdom of God, and all these things shall be added unto you." This was a good verse, for when she married Dennis, she left behind all creature comforts and security to follow Jesus with her new husband.

In Elsie's life, I saw that if we make Jesus first, we are able to love others more freely and more devotedly. Matthew 6:33 became the watchword of the Kinlaw's life and family not only in prosperous times, but also in times of pain, uncertainty, and sickness.

In the last month of Elsie's life, she was confined to bed. Hospice had been called in, and we all knew that the end was near. Dennis had several preaching appointments that he felt he should take. When he went to Elsie to ask her what he should do, she replied, knowing that she could die while he was gone, "Go Dennis and tell them about Jesus!" He went.

Out of Elsie's love relationship with Jesus came many fruits. First of all, Elsie loved other people. She loved passionately and completely, and she loved in truth. Her commitment to speaking the truth never wavered. And to those she loved, she spoke about the central reality of her life. The central truth for her was Jesus, and she told everyone that she possibly could about the One who is Truth.

If a person saw her only occasionally or met her only one time, she would get right down to business and ask whether that one knew Jesus and whether he or she was living with a clean heart. She never minced words, and she never waited for a better opportunity. Her love relationship with the Lord Jesus was such that she talked about Him wherever she went and with whomever she met.

I remember countless times when Elsie shared with waitresses, servers, and clerks about the difference that Jesus can make in a human heart and life. She knew what a difference He could make because He had made such a difference in her own heart. She would share her love for Jesus in such a way that each person wanted her to return. Her sweetness, her honesty, and her overflowing love were an irresistible combination.

Elsie Kinlaw also lived a life of prayer. Whenever she had a quiet moment she would get out her prayer list and go to Jesus with the names on that list. Almost every person she met ended up on her prayer list, and she faithfully prayed for the person's salvation, sanctification, and surrender to God's call. She loved to pray and to challenge people to go into missions—to give their entire lives to God. Her dream of being a missionary to China was fulfilled in the burden that she carried for that country. In her last prayer journal is this statistic: "One out of every three people who go to hell today are Chinese." Her comment on that was, "We cannot ignore that sad statistic for the most populous nation of the world. China must be a major thrust for world missions." Until the end of her life, she prayed for the evangelization of that nation.

Her prayers also took the form of action. When she was First Lady of Asbury College, her prayer group prayed for, and got a burden for, the salvation of the children of Wilmore and High Bridge. Even though she had a busy husband, five children, and a stressful home to run, she took the time to take those little ones to Sunday School and church every week. Out of that ministry to those children came eternal fruit—children and families were saved and transformed because several women put their prayers into action.

She also prayed for small, seemingly inconsequential concerns. Perhaps her family had the opportunity to witness more miracles than others did. For instance, she prayed over her wardrobe, that every piece in it would be appropriate and bring glory to Jesus. Jesus was there— even in her closet.

She prayed over her children's and grandchildren's toys. When one of her sons, Denny, was a child, she prayed he would not lose his baseball glove, and he kept it until after he married. She prayed that all her grandchildren would be born in the daytime so the mommies would not be so tired in delivery, and they were! She prayed for safety for her sons-in-law and grandsons-in-law when they were traveling; she prayed for beautiful weather for wedding days.

To be quite frank, she prayed about everything; there was nothing too small and nothing too large to be taken to Jesus. I remember we children cringed a bit when Elsie said, "Let's just pray a minute" because we knew that minute would be a very long time. I remember as an adult, running into her room and asking her to pray for various requests. I knew she would pray with all her heart. Even at the end of her life, people asked her to pray over them, their spouse, and their children. Elsie knew that when we cry out to Jesus, He answers. She claimed that reality in her life and in the lives of everyone she knew.

All members of the Francis Asbury Society family have benefited from her prayers. She has prayed for every supporter, every meeting, and every evangelist. The FAS office personnel knew that if a meeting was coming, they had to get a list of those attending to Mrs. Elsie so she could pray for each one.

In her prayer journal we found this quote, "One life totally devoted to God is of more value to Him than one hundred lives which have not been awakened by His Spirit."

Elsie Kinlaw's life had been awakened by the Holy Spirit, and she lived in fellowship with Him. Because of His presence, the love of Jesus radiated from her life and drew all kinds of people to her and to her beloved Lord Jesus. She had ministry to people of all ages. Children loved to bring her gifts; college girls came to her for counseling; young mothers listened to her advice and challenges; couples and families modeled their relationships on hers; older women became prayer partners for families and for the world. Even during the last year when she was confined to her house, she had a worldwide ministry through love, through prayer, and through her life that so clearly reflected the Savior. The hundreds who came to her home-going Celebration testified to the way God had used her life in multitudes of ways to countless people.

Elsie Kinlaw's life was a sweet-smelling fragrance to God—a testimony of what God can do with one little woman who says one big "yes" to Jesus.

CPSIA information can be obtained at www.ICGtesting.com
Printed in the USA
LVOW071350210912

299712LV00001B/2/P